Practical Guide to the Teaching of English

AS A FOREIGN LANGUAGE

NEW EDITION

Robert J. Dixson

Published by
Regents Publishing Company, Inc.
2 Park Avenue
New York, N.Y. 10016

Printed in the United States of America

TABLE OF CONTENTS

CHAPTER I
GENERAL PRINCIPLES

The purpose of this book is to provide teachers with suggestions as to actual classroom procedure. Although some theory may be touched upon in the course of the writing, the book puts principal emphasis upon the practical side of teaching English as a foreign language. It deals, in other words, with the "how" of teaching rather than the "why." Recently there has been a great flood of books and articles dealing with a descriptive analysis of English as well as the application of various scientific principles to English teaching. These books and articles are often written in such technical language and are so obscure in composition that they merely succeed in bewildering the reader. It is time, therefore, that something of a more realistic and practical nature be offered to guide teachers in the everyday task of classroom teaching.

Still, even though our ultimate concern is with more practical considerations, we must first turn our attention to certain general principles underlying the various procedures which we shall recommend here. Even the simplest classroom techniques must derive from some basic principles. We also need for the purpose of our discussion a common background of terms of reference. These principles are not new. They are in no sense extreme. They represent what may be considered a present-day consensus of popular opinion on the subject.

A few years ago at an International Seminar organized by UNESCO (United Nations Educational, Scientific, and Cultural Organization) to discuss the teaching of modern languages, the following general principles were subscribed to by the majority of the delegates and are presented here exactly as they appear in the official UNESCO report of the conference*:

1. The approach to the teaching of all foreign languages should be primarily oral.
2. Active methods of teaching should be used as much as possible.
3. The greatest possible use of the foreign language should be made in the classroom.
4. The difficulties of the foreign language in the matter of pronunciation, vocabulary, and grammar should be carefully graded for presentation.
5. The teaching of a language should enable the students to develop their own skills, rather than provide information about the forms of the language.

The seminar further agreed that "the four fundamental skills to be taught are: understanding, speaking, reading, and writing, in the order named."

Let us take a moment now to consider briefly each of these five principles in turn. As already explained, once this background material has been absorbed, we shall be able to deal more intelligently with the practical phases of our subject, which is the purpose of this book—namely, the teaching of English *grammar*, the teaching of *vocabulary*, the teaching of *reading*, etc.

1. The first principle given above states that *the approach to all foreign language teaching should be primarily oral.* There would seem to be little quarrel with this statement anywhere in the world today. In some places, of course, teachers do not know enough English to follow any oral method closely. They themselves are not fluent in English

---

The Teaching of Modern Languages, p. 50, a volume of studies deriving from the International Seminar organized by UNESCO at Nuwara Eliya, Ceylon, August, 1953.

and thus hesitate to talk very much in class. Instead they fall back upon more traditional methods, using translation as the principal teaching technique and the mother tongue as the principal means of communication. Nevertheless, with the current use of language laboratory equipment, or with just a tape or cassette recorder, it is possible even for these teachers to present authentic language models to their students, while at the same time working to improve their own oral production of English.

In still other places, traditional teaching methods prevail for a wide variety of reasons. Classes in many public schools are too large to permit students to have sufficient oral practice. Oral teaching techniques generally require considerably more energy and enthusiasm on the part of the teacher than traditional methods. Administrative officials in many public school systems are often conservative by nature and thus resist change of any kind. A stereotyped examination at the end of the course, stressing translation and formal grammar, is still the rule in many school systems. A teacher under these circumstances has little choice but to prepare her students for this examination. She herself may speak English well and may be interested in training her students orally, but the course requirements and preparation for the standardized written examination make oral practice quite impossible.

Still, we may say that these cases are now the exception rather than the rule. The general tendency in the world today is to use the oral approach in teaching foreign languages. Even in conservative school systems—where traditional methods still dominate—we find some oral techniques being introduced.

The reason for these changes is, of course, obvious. World conditions have altered greatly in recent years. Radio and television, the telephone, and the airplane have brought nations closer together. In particular, American movies and American industrial products carry English to every corner of the world. English has now become *the* world language. People everywhere today want to learn to understand and to speak English. In many cases, they must use English in their daily work. Naturally they are impatient with outdated teaching methods which do not lead directly toward these ends. The days of learning a foreign language passively, through translation and reading only, have passed.

Some linguistic scientists would have us believe that this general change in methods and the current emphasis upon the oral aspects of language are the result of their studies. We encounter statements which claim that "the last fifteen or twenty years have indeed seen the dawn of what might be described as a new scientific era of language teaching." Such points of view are rather naive. Useful studies conducted in recent years in the field of phonetics tell us more about the exact nature of English sounds. But otherwise, nothing at all of any truly "scientific" nature has been established concerning the teaching of English or any other foreign language. There still remains no "royal road to language learning." And it will be a long time before one is found. We should keep in mind that language teaching is not a science. It never has been and never will be.

Classroom situations vary widely. In addition, there are countless personal and psychological factors involved in language teaching which are not subject to scientific analysis. What can science tell us about the learning process in general, or the part played by memory in language study, or the value of repetition and drill, or the many personality factors involved? If we wish to use terms loosely and call any practical, common-sense approach to language teaching "scientific," that is one thing; but we should not be misled into thinking that language teaching has recently become a science or that terms such as "scientific analysis" or "descriptive analysis," though frequently used, have any real scientific meaning when applied to language learning.

The changes that have occurred in language teaching in recent years are the result of the same powerful social, economic, and political factors that have affected our whole modern world so profoundly. The style of language teaching has simply changed in keeping with the times. The role of the linguistic scientists in this process has been secondary. Proof of this may be seen in the fact that Spanish, French, and German are still largely taught, at least in the United States and in Latin America, by the same methods that were in use twenty or thirty years ago. In addition to English, these languages have also been studied linguistically. During the same period, on the other hand, the teaching of English has advanced considerably, in response to changing world conditions and the growing importance of English as an international language.

2. The second principle states that *active methods of teaching should be used as much as possible*. If we accept the first principle that the approach to language teaching should be primarily oral, then this second principle follows almost as a corollary. In any oral system, the aims are to teach the student to understand and to speak English. Students therefore must be given considerable oral practice. The teacher must naturally initiate and direct this oral practice since it cannot possibly originate spontaneously. With traditional methods of language teaching, the teacher could often sit back while students translated at their desks or did work at the blackboard. Word study and reading merely involved translation. All explanations of grammar or points about which the students had doubts were made in the native language.

In the oral approach, however, the teacher must participate actively in almost every phase of the lesson. She must provide oral drill on all aspects of the grammar. She must teach new vocabulary not by simply translating, but by using pictures, pointing at objects, performing actions, or making explanations in English. She must always be careful to keep within the vocabulary range of her students. She should use reading not merely as a passive exercise in understanding but as a source of conversational material as well. She should ask questions on the text. She should lead the class into whatever conversational channels may occur to her. She should continually correct faulty pronunciation. She should vigorously urge her students to develop correct habits of grammar and speech.

As may readily be seen, use of these oral techniques result in a rather active lesson. The whole atmosphere of the class is quite different from that of the traditional language lesson where passive methods prevailed. Since we shall return to this theme in later discussions, there is no need to develop it further at this point.

3. The third principle states that *the greatest possible use of the foreign language should be made in the classroom.* This third principle again follows logically the acceptance of the first two principles. If we are to use an oral approach to language to give the student as much practice as possible in understanding and speaking English, then English should naturally be the principal means of communication. Occasionally the teacher may wish to use the native language to explain difficult points of grammar or to define words which cannot be explained readily in any other way. But otherwise she should use just English in her teaching.

The teacher should also require that students speak only English during the lesson, and she should enforce this rule strongly. It is of great psychological advantage if students feel that they are in an English-speaking environment where English is the sole means of communication. In this connection, the teacher should also use only English in such everyday classroom matters as calling the roll, calling upon students to recite, directing students in their various classroom activities, etc.

Both the oral approach itself and the use of English can be reinforced by audiovisual aids. The most commonly used textbooks in English as a foreign language are accompanied by tapes or records which can supplement regular classroom practice. Language laboratories can furnish either corrective or individualized study. The use of tapes or records also offers the student the opportunity to hear more native English speakers than he might otherwise come into contact with in his classroom. We shall discuss language laboratory techniques in greater detail below.

4. The fourth principle states that *the difficulties of the foreign language in the matter of pronunciation, vocabulary, and grammar should be carefully graded for presentation.* This would seem on the surface to be a statement of very obvious fact. Certainly no one would be

foolish enough to present difficult subject matter first, followed by more elementary material later. The reference here, however, is again to outdated textbooks and teaching methods which gave relatively little attention to the matter of grading. These texts and methods emphasized reading and translation. The vocabulary was much greater in range than that used in an oral method. Careful grading was not important since no active use was made of the many words studied.

Similarly, grammar was studied passively through the simple device of translation. Since students were seldom required to use any of this grammar orally, there was no need to follow any particular order in presenting it. If the student merely understood the grammar, that was sufficient.

In the oral approach, however, grading becomes a matter of primary consideration. The vocabulary studied must be limited in range so that students can learn to use it with facility. This vocabulary should be of proven, practical value. The grammar must also be simple and practical. It must be presented in such a way that students can grasp it easily and make immediate use of it in speaking. Pronunciation likewise should be taught by a simple and progressive method.

With an oral system, unless all materials are very carefully graded and limited, the load which the student carries soon becomes too great for him. He becomes overwhelmed by his materials and is unable to cope with them orally. The whole system then breaks down. Naturally this is a situation which the classroom teacher should try to avoid. In some cases, the teacher herself may be at fault in this situation. The materials in the textbook may be carefully graded, but the teacher supplies them to her students too rapidly. She teaches too fast and fails to provide for sufficient oral practice and repetition. This happens particularly when a teacher's native language is English. Since the subject matter is so very simple for these teachers, they are often unaware of the real difficulties of English for the foreign student. Thus they tend to teach far too much and much too fast. This naturally nullifies all efforts on the part of the textbook writer to grade materials carefully.

5. The fifth principle states that *the teaching of a language should be considered more as the imparting of a skill than as the provision of information about the forms of the language.* A skill is an ability developed through prolonged practice and repetition. Playing the piano is a skill. Typing is a skill. Such skills, since they must operate almost automatically, take a long time to develop. They require continuous practice and drill. A knowledge, on the other hand, is a body of information acquired through extensive reading or investigation. Thus we gain a knowledge of history, of philosophy, or of literature through an extended study of these subjects. No particular skills are involved here.

Traditionally, foreign languages were considered as subjects for extended study rather than as materials for practice or use. The methods which were employed in teaching mainly followed the methods used in teaching the classical languages, Latin and Greek. Literary subject matter was preferred to colloquial forms. Translation and analysis, through the medium of the mother tongue, was the accepted approach. The student acquired a knowledge of his subject, important for its social and cultural implications, rather than a skill in *using* the subject matter.

Today, as we have already explained, the emphasis has shifted. Because of a general change in world conditions, we now study foreign languages in order to be able to use them in our everyday life. Our aims are immediate and practical. The new approach to language learning, moreover, considers language as a dynamic activity rather than as a body of passive information. We learn to speak by speaking, not by studying abstract grammar forms, reading the classics, or extensive translating. Furthermore, slow, labored speech, the result of translating from the mother tongue, is not acceptable. Language should be spoken freely and easily, even if it is limited in range. It should proceed almost unconsciously from carefully established habits. It should operate, in other words, as an acquired skill.

As with any skill, efficient use of a foreign language can be gained only through extensive practice. The present-day teaching methods which will be described in this book put great stress upon providing students with this particular kind of oral practice.

CHAPTER II
THE STUDENT AND THE TEACHER

We have essentially been concerned up to this point with definitions. There remain two other terms to be clarified. Before we can proceed with our discussion, we must first understand *about whom we are talking* and *to whom we are talking*. The two additional terms which we must define, therefore, are *student* and *teacher*.

The student is obviously the individual who is studying English. But this is not the point. We wish to call attention to the diversity of circumstances in which this individual may be studying English:

1. There is the young student studying English as a second language in an elementary school in Europe or Latin America.
2. There is the older student studying English in a high school in Europe or Latin America.
3. There is the student studying English, either in elementary or high school, in the Far East. Here the way of life, the customs, the culture, and the language concepts are so different from those of Western culture that the whole approach to English teaching must be greatly modified.
4. There is the student in India or Africa—where many languages and dialects exist—who is studying English as a means of communication in his own country, since his native language may not be the same for everyone.
5. There is the university student in a foreign country who is majoring in science and studying English for its technical value.

6. There is the foreign university student who is majoring in English.

7. There is the foreign student, at various levels, who is preparing to be a teacher of English.

8. There is the student, adolescent or adult, who is studying English in one of the special English teaching centers sponsored by the United States government throughout the world.

9. There is the student who is studying English at an American, Canadian, or English university and taking an intensive course in English for four or five hours a day in preparation for matriculation as a regular university student.

10. There is the adult migrant, one of thousands going each year to Australia, Canada, or the United States, who needs immediate and special training in English.

This list is a mere sampling. It could be extended, of course. It is presented here just to emphasize the tremendous amount of English study occurring in the world today. It also indicates that the circumstances of and reasons for studying English vary widely.

No writer attempting to discuss or write about methods of English teaching can possibly hope to cover this broad field completely. The only thing that can be done is to speak in general terms. Moreover, every writer must write from his background, drawing upon his own personal experiences. The teacher using this or any comparable book must continuously adjust everything she reads to her own circumstances. She should not reject a writer's views because they do not apply immediately to her particular situation. There may be incidental information which will prove of value to her. By the same logic, she should not blindly accept every recommendation which comes to her from an outside source.

A good deal of confusion exists today in the English teaching field because methods which are effective in one situation are often forced upon teachers working in quite different circumstances. Such methods may come well recommended, even carrying some semi-official or university stamp. But there is no guarantee that they will be effective in all circumstances. No one method of teaching yet exists which is so good that it has universal approval or application.

In the modern world, with its rapid forms of communication, the oral approach to language teaching, as outlined in this book, seems the most practical and serviceable in the largest number of circumstances. For this reason we recommend it here. Yet we should be aware of the fact that there are thousands of people all over the world who are still studying English successfully by quite different methods. All teaching materials and methods should always be judged as to their value in the immediate school or classroom situation. This should be a guiding principle for all teachers and administrative officials.

The second term we would like to discuss is the *teacher*. There are, of course, teachers for each of the English classes mentioned above. These teachers naturally vary widely in character. However, we are interested here simply in making a distinction between two main groups of teachers: *a.*, the non-English speaking teacher who herself has learned English as a second language; and *b.*, the teacher whose native language is English. In the pages which follow, certain remarks will be addressed to the second group.

a. The non-English speaking teacher forms, obviously, the larger group. It is this teacher who is involved with most of the English teaching going on today throughout the world. Since this teacher has studied English herself in the same way that her students are studying, she understands their problems. She herself knows very well how difficult it is to learn a foreign language. She teaches slowly and well, being careful at all times to keep within the vocabulary range of her students. In this respect she is a good language teacher.

In other respects, however, she may show obvious weaknesses. She may either speak English fluently or she may speak English haltingly and with great difficulty. If a teacher herself cannot speak a language well, she can hardly be expected to teach her students to speak well. Such a teacher withdraws into a kind of embarrassed silence. In class, she employs teaching methods where oral English is not required.

What can be done in this situation? Actually, if a teacher so wishes, she can learn to speak English at the same time that she teaches her students to speak. By following the various oral techniques recommended in this book, she herself can gain considerable oral practice while she carries on her regular classwork each day. Out of each daily class hour, the teacher will speak for perhaps thirty minutes. In time, if a teacher teaches four or five class hours daily, this amounts to considerable oral practice. Such practice cannot fail to benefit a teacher, particularly if her practice is checked against tapes or records which will give her a standard of pronunciation.

Sometimes a teacher hesitates to do much speaking in class because she feels that her pronunciation is inadequate. She is afraid that her own imperfect pronunciation may have an adverse effect upon the pronunciation of her students.

The teacher should make every effort to improve her own pronunciation, but at the same time she can easily counterbalance her own defects by making use of language laboratories. Records and tapes covering all phases of English pronunciation are available today. The teacher can use these both for herself and for her students. In addition, almost all texts now are provided with supplementary records or tape recordings. Particularly in cases where the teacher has a poor oral command of English, these audial aids should be made a regular part of the teaching program. Even where the teacher's oral command is good, language laboratories offer the student the opportunity to hear English spoken by a number of different speakers. They also provide the opportunity for the weaker students to do corrective work, and for the stronger students to go ahead more rapidly than the rest of the class.

Finally, this teacher should keep in mind that experience shows us that the acquisition of good pronunciation is a long and complex process, despite what some authorities may say to the contrary. Pronunciation is not an isolated part of language. It is closely related to every other phase of language. Rhythm patterns, for example, grow directly out of the grammar of a language. The sounds of a language, furthermore, are not constant or static. They are continually shifting and changing in value. Such aspects of language are not easily or readily learned. Noticeable improvement in pronunciation does not occur from one month to another or even from one semester to another. Consequently, students will not be greatly harmed—over limited periods of time—by studying with a teacher whose pronunciation is faulty, any more than they will benefit —within the same period of time—by studying with a teacher who speaks English natively, especially if this teacher is untrained in accent correction techniques. Many students study with English-speaking teachers for years without showing any real improvement in pronunciation.

b. The teacher whose native language is English naturally has many things in her favor when teaching her own language. She controls the grammar and idiom of the language without conscious effort. Her pronunciation is correct. She speaks with that ease and fluency which is usually common only to native English speakers. Non-English speaking teachers envy her; students prefer to study with her. Within the foreign area where she is working, she becomes an important person, a kind of local celebrity. Certainly it is both a pleasure and a privilege to study with a teacher who speaks a foreign language natively—provided, of course, the teacher is trained in this kind of teaching.

A certain number of English-speaking teachers working in foreign countries are trained to teach English as a foreign language. They are serious students of language. They are experienced teachers, or at least university graduates, with a background of preparation in methods of teaching, phonetics, and associated studies. They have gone to the foreign country expressly to teach English. Many Englishmen who have gone to Africa, Asia, and the

15

Far East in the last fifty years have made outstanding contributions to the field of teaching English as a foreign language.

This type of teacher, unfortunately, forms a relatively small minority. The greater number of English-speaking teachers working in foreign countries are amateurs. Their only qualification for the work is the fact that they speak English. They are the wives of American businessmen, travelers, or individuals who have been stranded overseas. They are in the foreign country quite by accident. They know no foreign languages and have no serious interest in language study.

Some of these teachers, although completely unprepared, are adaptable and inoffensive. Others, simply because English is their native language and the subject matter is therefore so incredibly easy for them, become experts overnight. They think they know exactly how English should be taught. They take a condescending attitude toward accepted teaching methods and materials. No textbook quite pleases them. Their teaching follows a kind of "free-wheeling" system; no attention whatsoever is given to the needs, abilities, or comprehension levels of the students. After four or five years of teaching experience, this type of teacher generally quiets down somewhat, but meanwhile she can be a real menace to the profession.

CHAPTER III
THE TEACHING OF GRAMMAR

The words of one language often bear some resemblance to the words of another language. However, in studying any foreign language, we soon discover that, in order to show function or number or time relationships, words are cast into quite distinctive forms in each language. These forms make up the grammar of a language. It is this grammar which forms the real basis of the language. It is primarily grammar structure that serves to distinguish one language from another.

Though these facts are generally recognized, no phase of language teaching has been so greatly disputed as the teaching of grammar. There are those who favor a strong grammar program, with a direct, conventional approach to the subject. Others favor an indirect grammar program, with emphasis on examples and only a minimum of explanation. Finally, there are those who reject the teaching of grammar altogether.

I

The argument and confusion concerning the proper place of grammar in foreign language teaching have resulted in part from the varying interpretations of the meaning of grammar by different groups. Let us examine some of the more common points of view.

A. *Old and New Concepts of Grammar*

In speaking of grammar, most people think in terms of what is now usually described as "formal grammar." This is the grammar which they themselves studied in school. These people speak English natively. The grammar which they have studied is therefore concerned strictly with analysis of the language. Typical English sentences are put on the blackboard and broken down into component parts. Each word is classified in terms of part of speech and usage (parsing). The structural arrangement of the sentence, including description and function of each modifier—word, phrase, or clause—is studied (diagraming). Latin terms and concepts predominate. Careful distinction is made between accepted forms and those which are considered vulgar or non-acceptable.

Obviously, this is a different kind of grammar from that which the foreign student needs and should study. The foreign student learning English is interested in assembling its many elements into forms and patterns which he can use. His approach is therefore one of synthesis rather than of analysis. He can hardly be expected to analyze in detailed form a language with which he is not yet familiar.

The foreign student studies the formation and the usage of the various verb forms in English. He starts with the simplest and then goes on slowly and laboriously to those that are more complicated. A knowledge of such purely elementary facts is taken for granted in the study of formal grammar. The foreign student wants to know how to use the different prepositions in English. He must learn how to turn sentences into negative form and how to ask questions in English. He needs practice in the use of such simple idiomatic verb phrases as *used to* ("I *used to* play the violin") or *to be supposed to* ("The train *is supposed to* arrive at three o'clock"). Considerations such as these receive no attention whatsoever in a formal grammar textbook. It is simply assumed that everyone who speaks English natively uses all these forms instinctively.

In short, the grammar which the foreign student studies and the grammar which the native speaker studies are two different things. The foreign student studies functional grammar or *grammar as language;* the native speaker studies formalized grammar. The two studies have little in common and overlap in only a few places. They really form two quite distinct subject matters. However, many people are unaware of these facts or prefer to overlook them. When grammar is mentioned, they continue to think in terms of the formal grammar which they themselves studied in school. For this reason they take the position that the study of grammar is of little practical value to the foreign student.

The study of formal grammar may not be useful to foreign students. But functional grammar, laying stress on the elementary structures of the language, is as essential as the study of vocabulary, pronunciation, reading, and any other phase of language. It provides a basis upon which the foreign student can build. Without the guidance which grammar gives him, the student is adrift on a vast sea of complex language forms which makes little sense to him. Functional grammar serves to reduce these forms to set patterns. The student studies these patterns and learns to master them. In this way he becomes able to increase his understanding and use of the language.

Experienced teachers are thoroughly convinced today that a study of functional grammar is indispensable to the foreign student. Systems of teaching languages such as the "Conversational Method," the "Inductive Method," the "Natural Method," where grammar is not used, show obvious weaknesses. Attempts to patch up such systems by an indirect or disguised use of grammar are also unsuccessful. The student must understand clearly what he is studying before he can be expected to proceed intelligently.

A capable British writer in the field of language teaching, Mr. I. Morris, after surveying the whole area of argument for and against grammar teaching, concludes:

1. A consideration of grammar is imperative; it dare not be left to look after itself.
2. A systematic course calls for grammatical progression concurrent with vocabulary progression.*

---

* *English Language Teaching,* Vol. XIV, No. 1, p. 23.

An American writer, Mr. C. Handschin, takes the same position. The following quotation from his *Methods of Teaching Modern Languages* summarizes present-day opinion on the subject very well:

". . . finally the student must have a systematic knowledge of grammar. He cannot remember the multitudinous facts except in groupings governed by principles. These latter must therefore be learned just as thoroughly as the individual facts. Indeed, the student is just as helpless if he does not know the laws (rules)— although he knows many concrete instances—as the student of the old school who knew the rules but scarcely any concrete instances. With all our advocacy of direct method in grammar, then, we recognize fully that finally the rules must be securely grasped and retained, though on the basis of acquired linguistic habits, not on that of pure memory work."[*]

B. *Grammar Learned Naturally in the Way a Child Learns the Grammar of His Native Language*

The teaching of grammar also fell into some disrepute during the period when the "direct method" of teaching language was first introduced. The direct method was widely acclaimed as a great step forward in foreign language teaching. The mere rejection of the mother tongue in all classwork and the exclusive use of the foreign language were expected to solve most language teaching problems. The direct method is not, strictly speaking, a method of foreign language teaching. It is, rather, a principle, which can operate through various possible methods.

Teachers, however, seemed to overlook this fact. They were enthusiastic. They felt that at last they were really teaching a "living language." A living language flourishes best in natural, everyday circumstances. Consequently, teachers were inclined to believe that the more closely the conditions of the classroom could approach those of the foreign environment—particularly the home—the more

[*] *Methods of Teaching Modern Languages,* p. 184, World Book Co., New York, N.Y., 1940.

20

easily and quickly their students would pick up the foreign language. From this position it was just a short step to the notion that a student best learns a foreign language by following the natural methods a child uses when he learns his native language.

Accordingly, in many direct method classes, not only was the use of the mother tongue forbidden but all teaching techniques not based directly upon the natural way a child picks up his native language were also rejected. Grammar study was abandoned. Many dependable classroom disciplines—drill, repetition, word study, formal review, memorization—were discarded. Grading of materials was not considered important. The results, as might be expected, were very often not as successful as had been anticipated. The direct method was a definite step forward in the sense that it served to draw attention to the importance of using the foreign language orally in class. But, as interpreted by some extremists, it set foreign language teaching back many years. We are still recovering today from the strong reaction during this period against the use of many traditional and worthwhile classroom teaching techniques and materials.

The two major fallacies which influenced the thinking of this period were based on the beliefs that classroom conditions could resemble those of the home and that the child is naturally a good language learner. But the classroom is not the home, and the conditions of the classroom are in no way comparable to those of the home. The classroom is not a place simply for fun and games. Students progress in a subject matter only by studying it seriously. The atmosphere of the home is friendly, informal, maternal. Time is of no importance.

The classroom, on the other hand, is a highly conventionalized situation. It exists for one purpose only—to give students concentrated and intensified experience in the various fields of learning. In the study of foreign languages, particularly, time is a very important factor. The only contact which most students have with the foreign language is in the classroom. The course, therefore, should be carefully organized. Only those teaching methods which are consistent with these facts should be employed.

The child, contrary to popular opinion, is not a particularly good language learner. Consequently, there is little reason why—in studying or teaching a foreign language—we should try to duplicate the "natural" manner in which a child learns his native language. The method which a child follows in picking up his own language is an excellent method—*for children*. But it is not a practical method for mature students. The mature mind is capable of analysis, concentration, observation, memorization. It possesses many qualities which are still undeveloped in the mind of the child. In learning a foreign language, we would be foolish indeed not to take advantage of these important attributes.

The child learns his native language well and easily because the circumstances in which he acquires the language are exceptionally favorable. The child spends his whole day in the atmosphere of the language he is learning. At home, his mother and family are always present to guide him. Outside his home, his playmates, with whom he must communicate, provide another stimulus. The child learns in a real language environment, with real things happening constantly all around him. Every effort at speech which he makes is rewarded immediately by the satisfaction of expressing himself, stating his needs, and getting what he wants.

The mature student, learning a foreign language in high school or college, studies under quite different circumstances. He enjoys none of the natural advantages held by the child. He studies in a schoolroom atmosphere which is sterile and unreal. He has no outside experience with the foreign language; his contact with the language he is learning is purely incidental. Thus, whereas the child enjoys maximum opportunity to repeat and memorize everything he hears, the mature student suffers from the strong tendency to neglect and forget everything he studies. Dr. Michael West, a highly respected authority in the English teaching field, states it this way:

"The picker-up is using the language off and on all day and every day so that he is constantly being reminded; his loss by forgetting is very small compared with the classroom child who has one class period with all the rest of the day to forget it in, and all Sunday as a help in forgetting the week's work, and periodical holidays and vacations to ensure the maximum possible loss."*

When a young child studies a foreign language only at school and has no outside experience with the language, he shows no more natural ability for learning a language than for learning mathematics, geography, history, or any other elementary school subject. The older student, studying in similar circumstances, makes much faster progress. The writer has had occasion to examine many young elementary school students now studying Spanish in the lower grades of certain public schools in the United States. Classes in which these students study are part of a large experimental program now being carried on in several American cities; it is designed to teach foreign languages to very young children. These young students, starting in the first or second grades, go on studying Spanish (or French) for several years. They have a short period of language study each day (20 minutes) or a few regular classes each week. The classes are not formal lessons. Yet the students are fully exposed to the foreign language. Direct methods of teaching are used. The teachers speak Spanish natively or, when such teachers are not available, the lessons are piped into the classrooms through loudspeaker systems.

However, even after several years of study, these students show very little advancement in their knowledge or use of Spanish. They have learned a limited amount of vocabulary, but they cannot use this vocabulary to form even simple Spanish sentences. In no sense can it be said that they understand Spanish when it is spoken to them. Their ear (auditory reception) is not particularly good. Their pronunciation is by no means accurate.

We have no wish here to criticize the teaching of Spanish in the lower elementary grades of these schools.

* *English Language Teaching*, Vol. XIV, No. 1, p. 22.

23

The program is still largely experimental. We simply want to emphasize the point made earlier that, contrary to popular opinion in the matter, the child possesses no special or innate capacity for language learning. Older students, studying in the same or comparable circumstances, inevitably make much greater progress. Dr. West, who was quoted above, summarizes the situation as follows:[*]

"—there remains a very widespread popular belief that the young child is a particularly gifted language-learner as compared to the later beginner. Parents point to the remarkable way in which the young children of Europeans in India or Africa "pick up" the native language. . . .This phenomenon is due not to the special aptitude of the child but to the exceptionally favourable circumstances of his learning; the older learner would, with his more matured intelligence and learning ability, excel if he were given the same circumstances; *but* he seldom is."

C. *Inductive or Deductive Methods of Teaching Grammar*

In the literature of foreign language teaching, one reads a great deal about inductive and deductive methods of teaching. *Induction* means a process of learning or teaching whereby numerous examples of a certain principle are presented and the rule is then inferred from these examples. *Deduction* means starting with the rule and then offering examples to show how the rule applies.

In various direct methods of teaching, where grammar is not taught, great emphasis is placed upon the inductive method of learning. Under these systems, for example, neither the use nor the formation of the various tenses in English is explained. It is assumed that, just as the child learns his tenses without formal study, the mature student will come in time to understand and use these tenses correctly through more exposure to the language. As has been pointed out, however, the important element of time enters here. The child has his entire childhood in which to learn

---

[*] *The Teaching of English as a Second Language*, p. 51, Macmillan & Co., London, 1945.

his native language, whereas the mature student has only a few lessons in class each week.

Many other factors also operate to make the two situations quite different. It is rare indeed that a foreign student gets enough practice through mere conversation to understand the use, for example, of the present perfect tense in English. Hundreds of examples must be given, and even then the student may fail to see any relationship between these examples. It seems simpler and wiser, under these circumstances, to explain the rule first and then to give these examples later. Once a student understands what he is doing and what he is supposed to learn, it is much easier for both him and the teacher to proceed.

In modern language classes, where the teaching of functional grammar forms a definite part of the program, the issue as to whether an inductive or deductive method should be used ceases to be important. Either induction or deduction may be used, almost indiscriminately. In teaching functional grammar, we may present reading material first. This material should contain examples that illustrate the new grammar rule to be studied. After reading this material, we then proceed to a statement of the rule itself, followed by practice exercises. This would constitute an inductive approach. Or we can start with the grammar rule itself, follow it with practice exercises, and then proceed to reading material where the grammar rule is applied in practical form. This would be a deductive process.

The inductive method seems to be favored in modern textbooks as being somewhat more interesting for students. It somehow appears to be easier to meet new material in context first, make the effort to understand it, and then proceed to a statement of the rule. On the other hand, there are many students who consider it easier to study the rule first and to proceed later to a study of its application.

Actually, as already indicated, it doesn't matter too much which method we follow. We can assault the grammar directly from in front (deductive method); or we can come up to it slyly from behind (inductive method). We can state the rule, let us say, on page 20 and follow it with the appropriate reading on page 22; or we can present the reading on page 20 and follow with a statement of the grammar on page 22. *In either case, the rule itself remains of minor importance.* An understanding of the rule on the part of the student *is strictly a preliminary step,* no matter how it is arrived at.

The real task, which still lies ahead, is to give the student sufficient oral practice with the rule so that he can make some practical use of it in understanding and speaking English. Here the teacher's role naturally becomes important. It is she who must provide this practice, control it, and direct it toward the proper ends. This practice, however, far transcends in importance any consideration as to whether the rule has been learned by inductive or deductive methods.

Experienced teachers of language know that it is fairly easy to teach the rules of grammar to a student, by one means or another. But knowledge of the rule constitutes merely a beginning. It is the drill work which follows that serves to implant the rule in the student's mind and give it practical application. As one goes on in the study of a foreign language and finally attains some fluency, the grammar rules tend to disappear, even from memory. But the practical forms remain. The correct forms begin to sound right to the ear. This of course is as it should be. When the correct forms of a foreign language begin to sound right, then one is well on his way to learning that language.

II

Assuming that the study of functional grammar should form a definite part of any modern and well organized course, how should we go about teaching this grammar? Here are some suggestions:

1. Most present-day English textbooks contain drill exercises based on whatever grammar principle is presented in the particular lesson. These exercises are of fairly familiar forms: some require the substitution of one word or phrase for another; others are of the multiple choice type;

others require a change in the verb form; still others call for filling in blanks, etc. If the textbook writer knows what he is doing, these exercises should be extremely simple and direct. Their purpose is not to trick the student or to find out how much he knows. They are designed simply to give the student practice with the rule under consideration.

The teacher runs over these exercises in whatever manner she thinks best. *The exercises should be repeated in one form or another several times.* Exercises should be practiced first with books open and then with books closed. Here the teacher presents the exercises orally, and the students follow the necessary instructions. All exercises may not lend themselves to this oral treatment, but many do.

2. The next step—and an important one—is for the teacher to provide special oral drills, supplementary to those in the text. Most textbooks offer a limited number of exercises. Limitations of space prevent the textbook writer from giving more than two or three simple sets of exercises with each grammar rule. Moreover, textbook exercises are very restricted as to style and variety. They help the student to understand the grammar principle involved but rarely do they generate oral practice of a natural, conversational kind. Very often students can do the exercises in the textbook perfectly, but are unable to use the grammar rule in conversation or free speech. The teacher, therefore, must provide students with sufficient supplementary oral practice to enable them to use each new grammar principle actively. No formal study of grammar and no textbook exercise can take the place of this oral practice.

Supplementary oral drills are very easy to devise and use. Once the teacher understands the general procedure, she can easily prepare oral drills to accompany each grammar rule that she is teaching. Here are a few examples of such drills:

a. Suppose a class is studying the negative form of the present tense. After the exercises in the book have been completed, the teacher says to the class, "Now I am going to give some additional *oral* practice in changing sentences to the negative form." She then gives the class a series of original sentences in the affirmative. The class repeats each sentence in the affirmative. On a cue from the teacher—either a hand signal or the word *negative*— the class chorally transforms the affirmative sentence into the negative form. The teacher may then want to ask individual students to make the transformations.

AFFIRMATIVE TO NEGATIVE

This same technique can also be used in teaching questions. The teacher gives a series of simple sentences to the

STATEMENT TO QUESTION

class, sentences such as "John speaks English well" and "They live near the park." The students change these statements orally to questions. If the class has already studied the negative form, the teacher can extend the drill to include the review of the negative form as well. Thus the student can *first* repeat the affirmative statement given by the teacher; *second,* change the sentence to the negative; and *third,* change the sentence to a question. Simple alterations of this kind can give variety or extension to any of the basic drills.

b. Suppose the class has already studied the simple present tense (John *speaks* English well) and is now studying the present continuous tense (John *is speaking* English now). The teacher can give the students a series of sentences in the simple present tense. The students change these sentences to the present continuous form. The teacher can reverse the process by giving sentences in the present continuous form; the students change them orally to the simple present tense.

c. Suppose the class has studied the present tense and the past tense and is now engaged in studying the future with *will*. The teacher gives a series of sentences in the present tense to the class. The students repeat each present tense sentence, then change it to the past tense and to the future with *will*. The teacher can add variety to the drills by presenting a series of past tense sentences with emphasis on such words or phrases as *yesterday, last week, last month*. The students then change these sentences to the future with an emphasis on *tomorrow, next week, next month*.

PRESENT TO PAST TO FUTURE

3. The oral drills outlined above are, as already mentioned, of a very simple and direct type, not too far removed from the usual textbook exercise. However, these supplementary drills generally contain original sentences, and they are also presented orally. This is the principal difference. The teacher can easily make such drills more elaborate as well as more interesting. These drills will still fulfill their basic purpose of providing students with oral practice on the grammar principle they are studying. Here are some slightly more elaborate drills. It should go without saying, incidentally, that all drills must be adjusted to the level and

ability of the particular class. A very elementary class cannot be expected to use drills beyond its comprehension. An advanced class naturally requires something rather challenging.

a. Suppose an intermediate English class has already studied the negative and question forms. Perhaps the students need to review these forms with some additional oral drills. The teacher asks a question involving some slight error in fact: "Does our English class begin at *eight o'clock?*"

CORRECTION OF FACT

The student first gives a negative answer: "No, Miss X, our English class doesn't begin at eight o'clock." He then follows with an affirmative answer and a correction of the facts: "Our English class begins at *nine o'clock*."

Then the student turns to the student sitting next to him and asks the same question that the teacher asked: "Does our English class begin at *eight o'clock*?" The second student answers in exactly the same way as the first student and then passes the question on to the next student. The teacher interrupts only when she feels the particular question has run long enough. Then she asks a new question.

Typical questions of this kind are: "Is February the *first* month of the year?" "Did Columbus discover America in *1493*?" One obvious advantage of this particular type of drill, which, incidentally, can be applied to many different grammar forms, is that the teacher's participation is relatively minor. The students do most of the talking. This is a very important consideration, since in most classwork the opposite situation prevails—the teacher does most of the talking. This is a very important consideration, since in most classwork the opposite situation prevails—the teacher does most of the talking while the students remain passive.

b. An interesting drill, as an example, can be used in teaching the idiomatic verb phrase *used to*. This drill serves not only to give practice with the phrase but also to show clearly the particular significance of *used to* in indicating a situation which existed at one time but no longer prevails.

For example, the teacher asks a simple question such as "Do you play tennis?" The student gives a negative answer first and then follows with a second sentence containing *used to*. In this case, the student answers, "No, I don't play tennis. But I *used to* play tennis."

The teacher's question to the next student might be, "Do you live on the west side of town?" The second student would answer, "No, we don't live on the west side of town. But we used to live there."

The third question might be, "Do you buy your clothes in Macy's?" The answer might be, "No, I don't buy my clothes in Macy's. I buy my clothes in Gimbels', but I used to buy them in Macy's."

Here again, instead of asking an individual question of each student, the teacher can prefer to direct the student to proceed as in the previous drill. The student, after answering the teacher's question, asks the same question of the student sitting next to him. This student answers and passes the question on to the next student, etc. The teacher interrupts with a new question only when she feels that the first question has run long enough.

c. In teaching an intermediate or advanced class *indirect speech,* the teacher can provide a natural and realistic drill in the following way:

After the class has completed the exercises in the textbook and understands the principles involved, she gives the class a series of simple statements. The students convert each of these statements to indirect speech. They simply begin each sentence with a phrase such as *"The teacher said. . . "*

Thus the teacher says to the first student, "Helen speaks French well." The student then converts the sentence to indirect speech: *"The teacher said* that Helen *spoke* French very well."

The teacher says to the next student, "I am going to Miami on my vacation." The student changes this to indirect speech by saying, "The teacher said that she *was going* to Miami on her vacation."

The teacher says to the third student, "John will be absent tomorrow." This student converts the sentence to, "The teacher said that John *would be* absent tomorrow."

The teacher continues in this way until everyone in the class has had practice in converting one or more such statements to indirect speech. Again, if the teacher prefers, she can have the first student, after converting the statement to indirect form, pass on this same statement to the next student, as done in the drills above. Thus, each statement is converted to the indirect form several times.

This kind of drill is invaluable in teaching students how

indirect speech actually operates. The rules in the book covering indirect speech sometimes appear rather complicated, but in actual use the students soon see how these rules apply simply and logically. Pronouns shift when a statement is changed from direct to indirect speech; and the verb tense often changes because the rule of sequence of tenses applies when the indirect speech begins with a past tense verb phrase such as *the teacher said.*

DIRECT TO INDIRECT SPEECH

Several variations of this drill on indirect speech are possible. In teaching indirect questions, for example, the teacher can ask the class a question such as "How old are you?" The student would convert the question to the indirect form in this way: "The teacher *asked* me how old I *was.*"

The teacher may also tell the students to convert the question to indirect speech by beginning their response with "The teacher *wants to know*. . . ." Thus, the teacher would ask, "Where is your notebook?" The student would convert the question to, "The teacher *wants to know* where my notebook *is.*"

DIRECT TO INDIRECT SPEECH

The students may also be directed to respond to questions with a statement beginning, "*I don't know....*" Thus, the teacher would ask, "How old is Mary?" The student would respond, "I *don't know* how old Mary *is.*"

Many such changes can be made on this simple basic technique. All are easy to use. All are extremely effective in

DIRECT TO INDIRECT SPEECH

getting over to the students the various principles of indirect speech.

d. The various conditional forms are easily taught by the use of supplementary oral drills. The teacher states some simple fact; the student repeats the teacher's statement and then adds an explanatory conditional clause. For example, the teacher says, "John doesn't prepare his lessons well." The student repeats "John doesn't prepare his lessons well," and then adds, ". . . but if he *prepared* his lessons well, he *would be* the best student in the class."

Or the teacher says, "I don't speak French well." The student responds with, "I don't speak French well, but if I *spoke* French well, I *would take* a trip to France."

The same procedure can be used to teach the past conditional form. The teacher says, "William didn't study before his exams." The student responds with, "William didn't study before his exams, but if he *had studied,* he *would have passed* his exams easily."

The teacher says, "Yesterday wasn't a holiday." The student responds with, "Yesterday wasn't a holiday, but if it *had been* a holiday, I *would have gone* to the beach."

CONDITIONAL

e. In teaching an advanced class the perfect form of the auxiliary verb *should* (i.e., *should have*), the following drills can be very effective. The teacher gives the students a series of statements which they are to consider as statements of error. The students, reciting in turn, correct these statements by using *should have* in the negative form and then *should have* in the affirmative form.

For example, the teacher says to the first student, "I sent that letter by regular mail." The teacher replies, "You *shouldn't have sent* that letter by regular mail. You *should have sent* it airmail."

The teacher says to the second student, "Mr. and Mrs. Smith drove to Mexico." The student replies, "Mr. and Mrs. Smith *shouldn't have driven* to Mexico. They *should have gone* by plane."

The teacher says to the third student, "We waited for you on the corner of 33rd Street." The student responds, "You *shouldn't have waited* for me on the corner of 33rd Street. You *should have waited* for me on the corner of 34th Street."

PERFECT FORM OF SHOULD

In this way, the teacher includes each student in the class. These particular grammar forms involving the use of *should have* and *shouldn't have* are generally difficult for foreign students to learn. Students tend to avoid them in everyday speech. This drill provides considerable practice with these forms. The practice has the advantage of providing a natural, conversational review.

A few words of caution: We have already mentioned that all such oral drills should be simple and clear in form. They should also be carefully adjusted to the comprehension level of the students. Nothing falls flatter than an oral drill which the students neither understand nor follow easily. Teachers, therefore, should experiment until they find a simple, effective drill *for each grammar principle studied.* This is not at all difficult to do. The sample drills given above are just a few chosen at random. The teacher can apply the same type of drill in many cases to other grammar principles. She can easily devise similar drills, or others quite original, to suit a particular class situation or to accord with her own teaching methods or personality.

Teachers who speak English natively can often supply on the spot the necessary introductory sentences for such drills. The teacher who does not speak English fluently will probably have to prepare such drills in detail beforehand, being careful to select only those sentences that fit the particular drill exactly. Teachers should keep a notebook with such drills ready for each day's work. Possible improvements in technique can be noted here as well as general remarks to help the teacher use the drill more effectively the next time it is tried.

Teachers should not hesitate to repeat such drills for several days running. Students learn from these drills much more readily than they do from materials in the textbook. It is interesting to see how students' faces often light up as they begin to do these drills efficiently. It doesn't seem to them that they are practicing grammar at all. They are simply using the language in a normal, everyday way.

4. Some teachers, for one reason or another, may not take kindly to supplementary oral drills and prefer other

methods of teaching grammar. However, it is difficult to see how anyone can fail to grasp the great utility of such drills. In any event, no one should restrict his or her teaching to one technique alone but should use any additional methods which serve to give the students oral practice in the use of the grammar being studied.

The *question-answer* technique is a dependable method of teaching all phases of language. Dr. H. E. Palmer, one of the best known of all authorities in the field of English teaching, writes: "Conventional question-and-answer work is the most effective of all the language learning exercises ever devised."* He goes on to say that the question-answer technique may be adapted as well for the teaching of grammar as for the teaching of conversation or any other aspect of language. The teacher simply asks a question; the pupil, *"borrowing most of or all the material contained in the question,"* answers it.

In using the question-answer technique for the teaching of grammar, the teacher asks a series of questions involving the particular grammar rule under discussion. Let us suppose the class is studying the idiomatic verb phrase *to be supposed to.* The teacher asks questions such as "What

TO BE SUPPOSED TO

This Language Learning Business, Palmer and Redman, p. 179, Harrap & Co., London, England.

41

time are you supposed to come to class each day?"; "Where are you supposed to meet your friend tonight?"; and "What time is the plane for Caracas supposed to leave?" Individual students give the answers to these questions.

Simple, everyday questions of this nature are easy to devise, easy for the students to answer. After the exercises in the text have been completed, and even before any supplementary oral drills are introduced, it is always a good idea to introduce students to the oral use of the grammar by asking some general questions of this nature, involving the particular grammar rule under discussion.

The only disadvantage of the question-answer technique, in the opinion of some teachers, is that the teacher-activity is very great as compared to individual-student-activity. In other words, the teacher asks a question and one student answers; the teacher asks another question and the next student answers. By the time the teacher has gone all around the class, she has spoken half the time and the students the remaining half. Now, let us suppose the class contains 30 students and, for purposes of argument, the grammar lesson lasts for a full hour. In this hour, the teacher has spoken for thirty minutes and the students for thirty minutes. But there are thirty students in the class. This means that each student has spoken for only one minute. Thus, the proportion of teacher-talking-time to student-talking-time is 30 to 1. This is a very high disproportion, especially in view of the fact that it is not the teacher who needs practice in speaking but rather the students. Moreover, such continuous activity on the part of the teacher can often be very tiring physically.

Language teachers have been confronted with this problem for many years. In any oral system of language teaching, the teacher is inevitably called upon to provide the major part of the activity. Yet there are several things the teacher can do to alleviate this situation, at least partially. *First*, the teacher can always proceed as was suggested for several of the oral drills described earlier. That is, she can ask the first student a question involving the grammar rule under discussion; the student answers this question and then turns to the student next to him and asks the same question again. This second student answers the question and then passes it on to the student next to him. The teacher interrupts to ask a new question only when she feels the first question has run long enough. This procedure has the obvious additional advantage of giving the students practice on the forms of questions as well as the answers.

Second, the teacher can experiment with having several students answer each question. That is, each time she asks a question, she requires that *five* students in rapid succession answer the question. For example, the teacher asks, "What time is the plane for Miami supposed to leave?" The first student answers, "The plane for Miami is supposed to leave at three o'clock." The second student gives the same answer, and so does the third, and so on.

At first sight, this may seem like a rather artificial means of forcing students to speak and of shifting the burden of activity from teacher to student. We must remember, however, that in an oral system of teaching, repetition of any kind is highly desirable. Furthermore, students catch on very quickly to what they are supposed to do. If the teacher, with a certain military discipline, insists that all five answers be sharp and brisk, the students will respond accordingly. In such a case, the technique works very smoothly and the results are highly satisfactory.

It was mentioned that *five* students in rapid succession answer each of the teacher's questions. The number *five*, of course, is purely arbitrary. The teacher can require that three students answer each question, or four students, or seven, as she prefers. Sometimes a classroom is so set up that the first student in a row answers, then the remaining students in the same row follow briskly with the same answer. The individual teacher can experiment briefly and then decide which system best suits her particular situation.

5. Another means of teaching language orally which is used rather widely today is the *choral method*. The choral method can be used to teach grammar as well as other

aspects of language. With this method, the teacher simply makes a statement to the class. The entire class repeats the statement in chorus.

The choral method is particularly good for teaching those aspects of grammar closely related to pronunciation or intonation. Thus, grammar forms such as contractions, verb tenses formed with auxiliary verbs, prepositional phrases, exclamatory sentences, and so on can often be taught rather effectively by choral means. With these grammar forms, the teacher emphasizes the rhythm pattern at the same time that she teaches the grammar principle. For example, in teaching contractions, the teacher might say, "He'll be back at six o'clock." She uses the normal conversational stress and rhythm patterns for the sentence, which the students repeat in unison.

The advantage of the choral method is that it increases student participation and reduces teacher-talking-time. *Each* student repeats each sentence the teacher presents. The disadvantage is that it is often difficult to know how individual students in a class of twenty or thirty are responding. The teacher may not notice mispronunciations or other errors. A few of the lazier students may not respond at all. They may simply move their lips to give the impression that they are participating.

To remedy situations of this kind, teachers often modify the choral method by calling on individual students *first*. That is, the teacher pronounces the phrase or sentence which she wishes repeated. Then she calls on two or three students *individually* to repeat what she has said. After these students have spoken in turn, the teacher gives the phrase or sentence a second time. Then the whole class repeats in chorus, possibly two or three times.

Teachers should experiment with the choral method to find out whether they like it and also to see in what form they may attain the best results. In general, the choral method needs both a strong guiding hand and considerable enthusiasm on the part of the teacher. It must be done well or not at all. In the hands of some teachers who seem to enjoy the role of choirmaster and thus contribute with the appropriate gestures, facial expressions, and so forth, the method turns out to be very effective. Other teachers feel somewhat uncomfortable using the choral method, and as a consequence they find the results less satisfactory.

6. Oral grammar, as well as other aspects of language, can also be taught effectively by what we may call (for want of a better name) the *prepared-seat-work method*. This method is really an extension of some of the teaching techniques already described above, particularly the *question-answer* and the *supplementary-oral-drill* techniques. With this method, all students in the class pair off; that is, they form groups of two students each. Previously prepared material, preferably mimeographed, is given to them. Using this material to guide them, the students drill one another on the particular grammar principle they are studying.

Let us suppose that there are twenty students in the class. They turn their chairs toward each other in groups of two if the chairs are movable; if the chairs are fixed in place, the students simply turn to face each other. In any case, they form ten groups of two students each. Within each group, one student proceeds to act as teacher, the other as pupil. Later they reverse their roles—the second student becomes the teacher, the first becomes the pupil.

Such a method needs very careful preparation. Teachers occasionally attempt to have students pair off or work among themselves in small groups, but the results are generally disappointing, if not completely disastrous. The discipline problem sometimes becomes very great. The advantage of the method suggested here is that everything is planned carefully beforehand. The students have already rehearsed what they are supposed to do and can then proceed without any difficulty.

The method should be applied in this manner. Let us suppose that the class has been using one of the supplementary oral drills suggested above dealing with indirect speech. The teacher has given the class practice with a series of some twenty questions which the students have converted to indirect speech by answering with a statement beginning with "I don't know . . . ." For example, the teacher asks the first pupil, "Where did John go?" The student answers, "I don't know where John went." The teacher asks the second student, "Does Helen speak French well?" This student answers, "I don't know if Helen speaks French well." And so on, through the whole series of sentences.

Indirect speech forms of this kind are difficult for foreign students and require considerable practice. The teacher asks enough questions of this type to go all around the class. She may ask some questions several times until all responses are sharp and automatic. When it is clear that the students understand the drill procedure as well as the grammar principles involved, she then directs the students to pair off. She gives each group a mimeographed sheet containing *the same twenty questions* which she has just practiced orally with the class.

The students then proceed as described above. That is, the first student in each group, acting as teacher, reads the twenty questions, one by one, to his companion. The companion converts each question to indirect speech by responding, "I don't know . . . ." When all twenty questions have been answered, the students reverse roles. The second student takes the sheet and asks the questions; his companion now becomes the student and converts each question to indirect speech.

This drill will take at least ten or fifteen minutes. The teacher meanwhile walks around among the various groups. She listens and offers suggestions or corrections. This same prepared-seat-work method can be used as a follow-up to any of the supplementary oral drills described above and also to any question-answer procedure.

Let us suppose the teacher has been using the question-answer technique to teach the comparative form of adjectives. The teacher asks the first student, "Which is larger, New York or Chicago?" The student answers, "New York is larger than Chicago." She then asks the second student, "Who is taller, John or Henry?" The student answers, "John is taller than Henry." The teacher goes all around the class, asking some twenty questions of this same type.

After the class has practiced these forms sufficiently, she directs the students to pair off. She then gives each group a mimeographed sheet containing the same twenty questions which the students have just practiced orally. The students proceed exactly as described above; that is, the first student in each group acts as teacher and asks his companion the twenty questions; his companion answers. The roles are then reversed; the second student asks the questions and the first student answers. The teacher meanwhile passes among the groups to listen and correct. The students themselves, however, provide the principal activity; it is they, rather than the teacher, who are now doing all the talking.

Some teachers may not have access to mimeographing equipment. In such cases, teachers can dictate lists of practice statements or questions to students. However, it is much better to use mimeographed sheets if at all possible. If the teacher has to dictate the practice sentences, she must make sure that the students have written the sentences correctly before they can begin the prepared-seat-work. Mimeographed materials are uniform. They also give a much more professional character to the seat-work. The teacher can pick up the mimeographed sheets at the end of each practice session, since the students have no further need for them. The teacher can file the sheets away in a folder, and thus they are ready for use the next time she teaches the same grammar principle.

7. The ever-present classroom blackboard can always be used to aid in teaching grammar orally and to provide students with supplementary practice on the particular grammar or idiomatic principle they are studying. If, for example, an elementary class is studying the formation and use of the past tense, the teacher can put a simple list of verbs on the blackboard in columns. The students are then directed to form two sentences with each verb, one sentence in the present tense and the second sentence in the past tense.

One list of verbs can be composed of regular verbs only. After the regular verbs have been studied, a list of irregular verbs can be put on the blackboard and studied. Later, when future forms are studied, the same procedure can be followed. A list of verbs is put on the blackboard; the students are directed to give three sentences with each verb—a sentence using the verb in the present tense; a sentence using the verb in the past tense; and a sentence using the verb in one of the future forms.

If an intermediate class is studying the formation and use of the past continuous tense (I *was studying*, etc.), again a list of common verbs can be put on the blackboard. Individual students first give a sentence using each verb in the simple past tense; then they give a sentence using the same verb in the past continuous tense.

For example, the first student starts with the verb *to study,* which happens to be at the top of the list. He uses the verb first in a sentence with the simple past tense, "I *studied* my English lesson last night." He then follows with a second sentence containing the same verb in the past continuous form, "While I *was studying* my English lesson last night, my friend called me on the telephone."

The next student gives two sentences with *to come,* which is the second verb on the list. Using the verb in the simple past tense, he says, "I *came* to school by bus this morning." He follows with a sentence containing the same verb in the past continuous, "When I *was coming* to school this morning, I saw a bad accident."

The teacher can easily devise many simple blackboard drills of this kind. These drills can provide practice on almost all phases of functional grammar. The teacher can also introduce drills of a more general type. These can sometimes extend over periods of several weeks. Let us use as an example a drill which gives continuing practice on the formation of the present and past tenses and the future with *will,* as well as with the negative and question forms of each of these verb forms.

The teacher puts on the blackboard a simple present tense sentence such as "John eats lunch in the cafeteria every day." She underlines the phrase *every day*. Underneath the words *every day*, she writes *yesterday*, and underneath that, *tomorrow*. The first student changes the sentence to the past and then to the future with *will*. He says, "John eats lunch in the cafeteria every day. John ate lunch in the cafeteria yesterday. John will eat lunch in the cafeteria tomorrow."

The third student changes the sentences to yes-no questions. He says, "Does John eat lunch in the cafeteria every day? Did John eat lunch in the cafeteria yesterday? Will John eat lunch in the cafeteria tomorrow?"

The fourth student changes the sentences to question-word questions. In this case, the teacher tells the student to begin each question with *What time*. The student says, "What time does John eat lunch in the cafeteria every day? What time did John eat lunch in the cafeteria yesterday? What time will John eat lunch in the cafeteria tomorrow?"

At this point, the teacher erases the sentence from the blackboard and puts a new sentence in its place. The students change this sentence and succeeding sentences in the same way they changed the first sentence.

If she wishes, the teacher can select sentences containing particular verbs which she wants the students to prac-

USE OF THE BLACKBOARD

49

tice. Each day she puts different sentences on the blackboard. The class can practice the drill over several weeks for ten or fifteen minutes daily. If desired, the teacher can make the drills more complicated by introducing additional verb forms. For example, she can add the present continuous tense (John *is eating* lunch in the cafeteria *now*) or the present perfect (John *has eaten* lunch in the cafeteria *many times*).

However, the advantage of the original drill as described above is its simplicity. Students have no difficulty in understanding what they are supposed to do. They are soon able to change sentences easily and rapidly to the past and future and also to convert them to the negative and question forms. If the drill becomes too complicated, the students may become confused. Their responses then cease to be rapid or "automatic," and the drill loses much of its value.

8. Some teachers use games to teach functional grammar orally. That is, by means of simple, repetitive devices, they give students pattern practice with various grammatical forms. Games naturally cannot be a routine part of the class program, but occasionally—for the last ten or fifteen minutes of a lesson which has turned out to be rather dull, or during the last class session of the week when the students are already thinking more of the weekend vacation than of learning English—games are quite welcome.

Frequently, such games are adapted from children's games played at home or in the lower elementary grades to teach other kinds of subject matter. Mr. R. A. Close, writing in *English Language Teaching,** suggests a game called "The Parson's Cat" which he and his brothers and sisters often played as children. His father always took the role of teacher, directing the game.

The game involves the repetition of a simple sentence, with each child making a substitution in the sentence. The first child, for example, begins, "The parson's cat is an *angry* cat." The word *angry* starts with the first letter of the alphabet, A. Therefore, the second child must substitute

*Vol. 14, No. 1.

for *angry* an appropriate word beginning with the second letter of the alphabet, *B*. Thus the second child says, "The parson's cat is a *black* cat." The third child substitutes for *black* a word beginning with the third letter of the alphabet, *C*. He says, "The parson's cat is a *clever* cat."

The game continues through the alphabet, with each child substituting a new word beginning with the next letter of the alphabet. Some of the responses may be absurd—these are not acceptable. Some may be humorous, and a good deal of innocent laughter results.

Another game suggested by the same author is useful in teaching the past tense, question forms, and new ·vocabulary. In this drill-game, the class first practices a standard, pattern-type sentence a few times. Then each student, reciting individually, repeats the sentence, substituting new vocabulary in the final phrase.

For example, this sentence is used: "I went to the supermarket yesterday, and what did I buy? I bought some *apples*." The second student repeats the same sentence but substitutes in place of the word *apples* the name of one object beginning with the second letter of the alphabet, *B*. He says, "I went to the supermarket yesterday, and what did I buy? I bought some *bread*." The third student repeats the sentence and substitutes the name of an object beginning with the third letter of the alphabet, *C*. In this way, the drill goes through the whole alphabet and, at the same time, through the entire class.

The writer has watched teachers use the following drill —in the form of a simple game—very successfully. Let us suppose a class has been studying the past tense of irregular verbs. The teacher puts on the blackboard a list of some fifteen or twenty common irregular verbs such as *see, take, bring, do,* etc. She then assigns each verb to a student. That is, each student *represents* a particular verb. The first student *is* the verb *to see;* the second *is* the verb *to take;* the third *is* the verb *to bring;* and so on.

Now the game begins. The first student, who represents the verb *to see,* says, "The past tense of the verb *to see* is *saw,* but I don't know the past tense of the verb *to get.*"

(Note that the list of verbs on the blackboard is not followed in order; it serves to guide the students only in a general way.) The student who represents *to get* then speaks up, "The past tense of the verb *to get* is *got*, but I don't know the past tense of the verb *to do*." The student who represents *to do* immediately replies, "The past tense of the verb *to do* is *did*, but I don't know the past tense of the verb *to sing*."

In this way, the students pass the different verbs back and forth among themselves. The teacher can encourage repetition. The students are very eager to recite when the particular verbs which they represent are mentioned.

This same game can easily cover other grammar forms. Instead of naming the past tense form of each verb, the students can be directed to give the past participle. The student would then say, "The past participle of *to go* is *gone*, but I don't know the past participle of *to take*." The student who represents *to take* would then reply, "The past participle of *to take* is *taken*, but I don't know the past participle of *to drink*."

This game can also teach vocabulary effectively, particularly such things as opposites. A list of common words which have easily recognized opposites (antonyms) is put

VERB GAME

The past tense of the verb *to go* is *went*, but I don't know the past tense of the verb *to eat*.

The past tense of the verb *to eat* is *ate*, but I don't know the past tense of the verb *to hear*.

The past tense of the verb *to hear* is *heard*, but I don't know the past tense of the verb *to know*.

on the blackboard. Each word is assigned to an individual student. The first student, who represents the word *large,* for example, begins, "The opposite of the word *large* is *small,* but I don't know the opposite of the word *fat.*" The second student, who represents the word *fat,* replies, "The opposite of the word *fat* is *thin,* but I don't know the opposite of the word *tall.*" The student who represents the word *tall* then replies, and the drill continues in this way through the entire list of words.

9. In the last few years, language laboratories have frequently been used to teach all aspects of language, including grammar. Almost all the standard English texts are provided with tapes which can be played on dual-track equipment. This means that the student has the opportunity both to listen to the tape and to repeat and record the material he hears on the tape; he can then play back the tape and listen to his own performance. The tapes that go with the various texts usually include all the grammar drills that appear in the texts themselves. In addition, there are several sets of tapes which give supplementary grammar drills.

Language labs are of course invaluable to the teachers whose own command of English is weak. For those teachers, it is advisable to schedule regular laboratory periods if the equipment is available. This gives the students the opportunity to hear English as it is spoken by native speakers. Other teachers can schedule lab periods when they feel it would be necessary or helpful. Almost all language laboratory equipment has some sort of monitoring device so that the teacher can check on the performance of the students. The monitoring should not be ignored; it gives the teacher an excellent opportunity to discover the strengths and weaknesses of individual students and to keep track of their progress.

For all students, language labs offer two particular advantages. The first is the opportunity to listen to themselves and to measure their production of English against a native speaker. The second is the chance to do individualized work, since the tape equipment will either permit the students to do special corrective work or to continue at their own pace according to their ability.

In addition to tapes, many texts also provide sets of records with material similar to the tapes. Records, of course, do not have the capacity for recording and playback that the tapes have; nevertheless, they can give the students the opportunity to do individualized work. They are especially valuable for home study, thanks to the prevalence of record players in the world today.

10. Certainly enough suggestions of a rather wide variety have been offered above to provide teachers with the means of teaching grammar orally. The teacher simply has to choose whatever drills or special techniques may interest her. She may also experiment and arrive at even better techniques of her own invention. Many drills serve particularly well for review purposes. However, we strongly recommend that the drills be used regularly, as an integral part of every grammar lesson. Such drills, of course, should never continue for too long a time during any one class session. There is no need to tire or bore the students. Ten or fifteen minutes should be the normal time limit for all such drills.

Some teachers may complain that some of the drills that have been described seem rather mechanical and dull. This is not the case at all. The drills are lively and interesting. Students inevitably enjoy them. It simply happens that the written explanations of such drills often become a little complicated. The drills themselves, when actually practiced by a class under the teacher's oral direction, are easy to understand and fun to do.

There remain a few fairly conventional ways of teaching functional grammar which we shall mention here briefly.

Dictation is a standard classroom procedure which can often be adapted to teach many grammar forms. For example, the teacher can dictate simple sentences to the class. Students then write these sentences not as dictated but in the negative, or as questions, or with a change of tense, etc.

Some teachers use *wall charts* very effectively to teach grammar. The teacher simply asks prepared questions

DICTATION EXERCISE

about the various objects on the wall charts. She phrases the questions so as to involve whatever grammar principle the class is studying.

Other teachers use *flash cards* to teach grammar. The teacher writes selected verbs or certain grammatical phrases on the cards. Students make up sentences with

WALL CHART EXERCISE

these verbs or phrases, or they convert the material to different forms, as the teacher directs.

Workbooks containing numerous grammar exercises to supplement the drills in the tests are now available with almost all the standard texts. These can be used either in class, if time permits, or at home as supplementary work.

CHAPTER IV
THE TEACHING OF CONVERSATION

In foreign language teaching, when we speak of teaching conversation, we do not refer to the kind of social conversation that goes on around the family dinner table or when friends gather. This kind of conversation is rarely achieved in any language classroom. The classroom, as previously mentioned, is a very artificial situation. There is little opportunity for any social activity of any kind. There is the teacher who alone speaks the language well—and twenty or thirty extremely passive students with only a fragmentary knowledge of the language. In addition, there are obvious limitations of time, space, and circumstance. The students must spend all of their time learning a difficult subject matter in the most intensive but practical form possible.

Under these circumstances, the best that we can hope for in the way of normal conversation is a simple exchange of greetings, remarks, or directions between teacher and student. The teacher, of course, asks numerous questions about the material the class is studying. The students answer these questions. The entire exchange takes place in the language that the students are learning. But this is the extent of the "conversation" which occurs.

Nevertheless, despite these obvious limitations, conversation forms an extremely important part of any modern language course. Conversation provides students with a means of expressing themselves. It is often the only actual practice which students have in using the foreign language. Consequently, it must be encouraged by every means possible. Teachers should not consider conversation as an incidental phase of language study, something which grows or takes care of itself as the student advances in the language. They should teach it by positive and active means, giving it the same attention or even greater attention than they give to grammar, reading, pronunciation, or any other aspect of language.

How does one go about teaching conversation to foreign students? Here are some suggestions:

1. The conventional question-answer method remains probably the most simple and direct method of teaching conversation in a foreign language. Although the method has minor disadvantages in that the teacher does a disproportionate amount of work and talking, the method has been used successfully for many years. The well-known Berlitz system relies almost exclusively upon a question-answer procedure to teach all foreign languages.

We have already discussed the use of the question-answer method in teaching functional grammar. The method is most effective, however, for teaching general conversation. Some simple reading material is used as a basis for study. The teacher asks a series of questions based on this material, and the students answer these questions.

The question-answer method is easy to use. However, for the best results, the teacher should keep in mind one or two very important points. The great advantage of the question-answer method is that the student, in answering the teacher's question, receives a certain amount of prepared material to guide him in his answer. In other words, the teacher's question, *if properly phrased,* provides the student with a kind of formula which he follows in constructing his answer.

For example, the teacher asks, "How long does it take you to prepare your English lesson?" The student answers, "It takes me two hours to prepare my English lesson." In his answer, the student follows the exact form of the teacher's question. In this case he simply changes the verb from the question to the statement form and makes the necessary changes in the pronouns.

In a more simple example, the teacher asks, "Who is the tallest student in our class?" The student changes only the first word in the sentence and replies, "John is the tallest student in our class."

Dr. H. E. Palmer, the great English authority and teacher, experimented extensively with the question-answer method. As mentioned earlier, he considered question-answer work to be "the most effective of all language-learning exercises ever devised." Palmer insisted, however, that if the technique is to be carried out successfully, all questions asked by the teacher must be carefully planned or thought out beforehand. Questions should never be haphazard, either in form or content. Specifically, Palmer insisted that any question asked by the teacher must be of a nature that admits the following:

  a. *an obvious answer,* not an answer that requires one or more complicated acts of judgment on the part of the student;
  b. *an easy answer,* not one that requires the use of words, facts, or constructions unknown to the student;
  c. an answer which is *to the point;* that is, a direct answer involving only a moderate change through a process of conversion, substitution, or completion of the material contained in the teacher's question.

Some teachers—especially those who speak English natively—tend to get rather tricky with their questions in using a question-answer technique. These teachers are not always aware of the great difficulty of learning a foreign language. They ask questions which are simple to them but complicated to the foreign student. The form of their questions, moreover, offers no help to the student in constructing his answer. These teachers often use vocabulary which is unknown to the students. This is an obvious abuse or distortion of the question-answer method. Question-answer teaching is effective only when the teacher phrases all questions simply and clearly and when the student can easily answer them in a precise, clear-cut way.

2. Many teachers use the question-answer method in teaching so-called *action chains*. Action chains represent a series of events or actions which the teacher presents in dramatized form. The teacher, in other words, "acts out" a simple series of related actions. Action chains are sometimes referred to as *lesson themes*. The teacher, for example, gets up from her desk, walks to the door, opens the door, closes the door, picks up an eraser, etc. As she performs each of these acts, she asks an appropriate question.

As she gets up from her desk, she may ask, "What am I doing?" A student answers, "You're getting up." As she walks to the door, she asks, "What am I doing now?" A student answers, "You're walking to the door." As she opens the door, she may ask, "Am I opening the door or closing the door?" And a student answers, "You're opening the door."

The teacher continues asking questions of this kind through an entire chain of perhaps seven or eight related actions. Later she may alter her questions and change to another tense. In this case, she may ask, "What was the first thing I did a few minutes ago?" A student answers, "You got up from your desk." She then asks, "What was the next thing I did?" A student answers, "You walked to the door."

The teacher may wish to give the students practice in the use of the present perfect tense, for example. Possibly the class has just studied this verb form. Thus, the teacher writes on the blackboard and asks, "What have I just done?" A student answers, "You've just written on the blackboard." The teacher then walks to the door and asks, "What have I just done?" The answer is, "You've just walked to the door." She then opens the door and asks, "Have I just opened the door or have I just closed the door?" A student responds, "You've just opened the door."

The question-answer method used in association with various action chains is a very old teaching method. It was first introduced by the Frenchman Gouin during the late nineteenth century. Gouin believed that all sentences in the foreign language should be "recited and acted at the same time." He argued, with considerable logic, that any action tends to drive home the meaning of the spoken word and to make it a reality. Under the Gouin system, students as well as the teacher were required to act out literally hundreds of related action chains.

In order to achieve successful results, the teacher must carry out the teaching of action chains with considerable enthusiasm. Otherwise, these action chains, especially if

ACTION CHAIN

they are repeated frequently, tend to become monotonous. Furthermore, the novelty of the method wears off after a short time, and the students then lose interest. Nevertheless, the general technique remains one which can readily be adapted to many different situations. It is a technique which any teacher can use on occasion in modified form. It works particularly well in teaching young children. Some teachers who have a flair for dramatized teaching enjoy going through action chains and therefore learn to use them well and easily. The teachers are able to apply them in interesting forms to various activities in and around the classroom.

3. The question-answer technique may be developed, if desired, into a complete teaching method, quite apart from its everyday use in teaching oral grammar, conversational forms, and other subject matter. When used in this way, the teacher can extend the technique to involve a great number of loosely related questions which she asks in a rapid-fire manner. These questions are based on some reading material, but the questions develop and multiply in whatever direction the teacher determines.

Let us suppose a question based on the reading material asks, "Was Mr. Brown a tall man or a short man?" The teacher asks the first student this question, but then proceeds to ask an additional dozen or more questions branching out from this original question.

For example, she may ask the second student, "Are you taller or shorter than your brother?" She may ask the third student, "Is Henry taller or shorter than John?" She moves all around the class, asking more and more questions of the same general type: "Who is the tallest boy in our class?"; "Who is the tallest girl in our class?"; "Is your father a tall man or a short man?"; "Is your mother a tall woman or a short woman?"; and "Are women generally taller or shorter than men?"

When this general theme has been exhausted, the teacher returns to the text. She asks the next question appearing in the text. Then, using this question simply as a point of departure, she again branches out into a second long series of loosely related questions. During the time allotted, the teacher may ask the class as many as fifty or sixty questions in this way. The technique works well where textual material is scanty or where there are too few questions in the text to give the students sufficient practice in speaking. The teacher should naturally prepare the questions beforehand, adjusting them accurately *to the needs as well as to the comprehension level of the students.*

This method obviously puts emphasis on the oral use of language. It makes use of the simple device of asking questions to keep students talking. In this respect, it is a useful teaching technique. Its obvious disadvantage is that many of the questions, even though the teacher has prepared them beforehand, tend to run rather far afield. Adult students will generally understand the teacher's purpose in asking multiple-form questions of this type. Younger students, however, begin to think that many of the questions merely sound silly. Consequently, they soon lose interest in answering them.

However, here again we may learn something from this technique, even though we may not wish to follow it in the exact form described above. It is clearly not imperative that we ask ten or twelve questions for each question appearing in the text; but in many instances, we can learn to ask two or three additional questions of a carefully controlled type. In this way, we provide the students with further practice in speaking. If the questions are generally interesting to the students, we also gain another advantage. The students feel that they are answering real, everyday questions rather than the usual dull, dry textbook questions. The atmosphere of the class becomes a little less formal, a little more friendly. Some simple conversation may even result. We shall see more clearly how this technique operates when we discuss the teaching of reading by the question-answer technique in the following chapter.

4. We mentioned above that the only negative feature of the question-answer technique in teaching foreign language is that the teacher sometimes does a disproportionate amount of work and talking. This point was discussed

previously in the chapter on *Teaching Grammar*. There was an example of a hypothetical class of thirty students studying under a question-answer method for a full class hour of 60 minutes. The teacher of this class asked questions for 30 minutes; the students answered for 30 minutes. That is, each individual student recited for only one minute of the class hour. This is obviously a high proportion of teacher-talking-time to student-talking-time.

One means of circumventing this difficulty is to have several students in succession answer each of the teacher's questions. This procedure applies equally well to the teaching of conversation as to the teaching of grammar. Each time the teacher asks a question, she simply requires that some of the students answer the same question in turn. The teacher does not repeat the question. The students, one after the other, simply repeat the answer. This naturally increases the proportion of student-talking-time to teacher-talking-time. The teacher may direct that *three* students answer each question in turn, or *four* or *five* students, as she decides. She may also direct that all answers after the first one be especially sharp and "clean."

This general procedure may seem at first glance to be a little artificial and a little monotonous for both teacher and student. However, we strongly recommend that teachers experiment with the method to see what results they can obtain. They should also keep the following points in mind:

a. First, in any modern language course emphasizing oral techniques, we always aim at as much repetition as possible of everything which is taught. Thus, it does the students no harm at all to hear the same answer repeated four or five times. In fact, it may help them to remember the sentence pattern more easily.

b. Second, the first student who answers the teacher's question will probably answer somewhat incorrectly. The teacher will have to correct the first student's answer. The other students repeating the answer must pay close attention to the teacher's corrections. Otherwise, they run the risk of also answering incorrectly.

c. Third, the technique may seem artificial or monotonous to a person who speaks the language natively. However, to the foreign student it still represents a formidable challenge to answer the teacher's question with absolute correctness, whether he is the first or the fifth student.

QUESTION/ANSWER TECHNIQUE

5. Another means of increasing student activity and cutting down teacher-talking-time, while still following a question-answer method to teach conversation, is through

the use of the *prepared seat-work method,* which was described in some detail in the previous chapter. This method can be used to teach conversation in much the same way that it is used to teach grammar. In general, it is a method which involves the careful rehearsal of certain procedures which the students follow later while working by themselves at their desks.

The average textbook contains various reading selections, followed by the usual series of ten or twelve questions based on the material. To prepare for using the prepared seat-work method for teaching conversation, the teacher first reads this selection aloud together with the class, giving explanations for all new words, correcting pronunciation, etc. The students then read the questions based on the selection and answer them. If she wishes, the teacher may next ask the same questions orally. The students answer with their books closed. In any case, the teacher assigns the material as homework and advises the students to practice answering the questions at home, *orally* if possible.

The following day, the teacher follows the same general classroom procedure. The reading selection is read aloud by the class. The students then read the questions based on the selection and answer them. The teacher next reads the questions orally, and the students, with books closed, answer them. At this point the teacher may read the same questions two or three times. Each time she asks the questions a little faster, until she finally feels that all the answers are not only correct but fairly "automatic."

The teacher next directs all the students to pair off, either by shifting their seats or simply by facing each other. One student of each group now assumes the role of teacher. With his book open and following the text, he asks the same questions just asked by the teacher. The second student of the group becomes the pupil and answers the questions.

Later, the roles are reversed. That is, the second student opens the book, becomes the teacher, and asks the questions. The first student closes his book, assumes the role of student, and answers the questions.

Meanwhile, the teacher walks among the various groups to check on the answers, correct pronunciation, etc. Little discipline is necessary because the students have been so carefully rehearsed on both the materials and the procedure that they know exactly what they are supposed to do—and, moreover, enjoy doing it.

This method has numerous advantages and few defects. Any teacher can use it at any classroom level from mere beginners to very advanced students. The materials are simply adjusted to the needs of the particular group. This method provides a great deal of useful repetition without ever once tiring or boring the students. The students go over the same material seven or eight times without counting homework preparation. Yet the work is broken down into two class sessions. Moreover, each step in the process varies the form of the repetition considerably. The result is that the students are seldom aware of the actual repetition taking place.

In cases where the textbook may not contain reading selections which can be used as described above, the teacher can simply supply the students with mimeographed sheets containing appropriate reading material. Any simple anecdote or short reading passage followed by the proper questions will serve for use with these sheets. The teacher distributes the sheets to the class for practice and study and picks, up them later for use with subsequent classes.

6. *Wall Charts* provide a very convenient means of teaching classroom conversation. Such charts are enlarged pictures of common, everyday scenes, such as a street corner, a restaurant, a home, a farm, etc. The teacher points to various objects on the chart and asks appropriate questions. The questions can be designed to provide practice with some grammar principle, new vocabulary, or whatever conversational forms the teacher may wish to emphasize.

The method is an old and simple one, but it is very effective in provoking classroom "conversation." Dozens and dozens of questions can be asked about each of the scenes pictured on the charts. After the students have had sufficient practice in answering these questions, the teacher can also point to various objects on the chart and ask the students to create four or five sentences about these objects.

Thus, on a chart showing a busy street corner, the teacher points to a policeman in the center of the picture. The student says, "That's a policeman. He's wearing a blue uniform. He has a whistle in his hand. He's directing traffic."

The teacher next points to a woman crossing the street. Another student says, "That's a woman. She's a young woman. She's wearing a large white hat. She's crossing the street." The drill continues in this way with all the important objects appearing on the chart.

When wall charts are not available, some teachers use posters or cut large pictures from magazines, which they mount on cardboard. They use these materials as a basis for conversation in the same way the wall charts are used.

The classroom map falls into the category of a wall chart and can always be used to provide some classroom conversation if no other materials are available. The teacher points to a foreign country on the map and asks simple questions about the country. "What is the name of this country?" "What is the capital of this country?" "Does this country have a large or small population?" The students can also be asked to volunteer simple information about each country the teacher indicates.

In a particularly good conversational drill with a wall map, the teacher points to some foreign country; France, for example. The student says, "That country is France. A man who lives in France is a Frenchman. The language which he speaks is French." The teacher then points to Spain. A second student says, "That country is Spain. A man who lives in Spain is a Spaniard. The language which he speaks is Spanish." The teacher continues in this way, pointing at different countries. The students follow the same pattern in giving appropriate information about each country. This drill can be continued for short periods during several class sessions.

MAP EXERCISE

7. The *Choral Method* is used today by many teachers to practice conversational forms. The teacher makes a statement to the class. The whole class repeats the statement in *chorus*. This method was essentially discussed previously in the chapter on *Teaching Grammar*. In using the choral method to teach conversation, teachers generally employ

materials such as dialogues or selections from plays where actual everyday conversation is presented. The teacher reads one line of text. She emphasizes the conversational pattern, the rhythm of each phrase, and the intonation. The students repeat in chorus, trying to follow exactly the manner in which the teacher has read the sentence.

Many teachers use a modified form of the choral method in somewhat impromptu fashion throughout the entire lesson. Each time the teacher considers a particular statement worthy of choral repetition, she gives a prearranged signal. The whole class then responds in chorus.

For example, let us suppose that the teacher is working with one of the simple action chains described above. She gets up from her seat, walks to the door, etc. As she performs each action, she asks an appropriate question. As she walks to the door, she asks, "What am I doing now?" One student, reciting individually, answers the teacher's question first. He says, "You're walking to the door." The teacher then signals to the class and the whole class repeats in chorus, "You're walking to the door."

The teacher next opens the door and asks, "Am I opening the door or closing the door?" An individual student answers, "You're opening the door." At the proper signal, the whole class repeats the response in chorus.

This technique may be used when the class is working with reading materials, exercises in the text, wall charts —in fact, whenever the teacher asks a question of any kind. One student (or two or three students if the teacher prefers) first answers the question individually. At a given signal, the whole class then repeats the answer in chorus. The advantage of all choral work is that it keeps the entire class active. It also gives the students more practice in speaking. Finally, since student activity is increased somewhat, it tends to reduce the normally high proportion of teacher-talking-time to student-talking-time.

8. The teacher may introduce some variety into the language lesson by using reading selections which are unfamiliar to the the students. This technique provides the class with considerable oral practice. Briefly stated, the

technique works in this way: The teacher selects some appropriate reading material from an outside source, reads it to the class, and quizzes the students on the contents. It can be something which the teacher reads from a magazine, an anecdote, or any simple narrative selection. Naturally, she should make sure that the material is carefully graded to the students' level and does not contain any grammatical constructions or idiomatic forms which the students have not yet studied. The selection may contain certain new words, but the teacher should explain the meaning of these vocabulary items to the class beforehand.

After the teacher has explained all the new words, she reads the selection aloud to the class. She may read the selection two or three times to be sure the students understand it. She then asks the class various questions—about the characters appearing in the reading material, what happened to them, where the action takes place, etc. The questions should be as simple and direct as possible.

Employed on occasion, this method provides a pleasant change from more routine classroom procedures. Moreover, students generally enjoy this type of exercise. The material is new and fresh. It is a great challenge to them to try to understand totally new material which is presented to them in oral form only.

9. Some teachers, while emphasizing at all times in every lesson the oral use of language, still like to set aside a certain portion of each class period exclusively for conversational purposes. Thus, they may set aside the last ten or fifteen minutes of each period to be used in this way. The students close and put aside their textbooks. The classroom atmosphere presumably becomes somewhat more relaxed and more conducive to the exchange of conversation.

In this brief ten or fifteen minute conversation period, the teacher may use any one of the following techniques:
  a. She may ask a series of general questions based directly on the materials in the text. These questions, while providing the students with practice in speaking, may serve at the same time as a general review of material the class has previously studied. A ten or fif-

teen minute review of this kind once—or even twice—a week can be useful to any class.

b. The teacher can ask the class a series of somewhat personal questions covering school or social activities. The subject matter is not important as long as the questions are of some interest to the students and provide a basis for simple conversation or discussion.

c. The teacher may read to the class a series of statements, each containing a single-word error. The students then discuss these statements orally. The students first restate the sentence in the negative; then

CONVERSATION EXERCISE

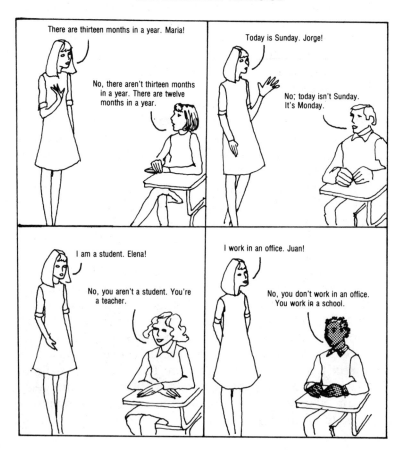

they state the sentence in the affirmative with a correction of the error at the same time. For example, the teacher says, "There are thirteen months in a year." The student replies, "No, there aren't thirteen months in a year. There are twelve months in a year." Other statements of error of this type are: The largest city in the United States is Chicago. Columbus discovered America in 1493. The third month of the year is April. The English alphabet contains twenty-seven letters.

d. The teacher may put on the blackboard lists of animals, for example. The first list may be a list of domestic animals. Sometimes the teacher may have pictures of these animals on a wall chart. In any case, she proceeds to ask simple questions about the various animals. After the class has practiced answering the questions, the teacher may also ask students to volunteer three or four "free" sentences about each animal. The teacher points at a cow. The student responds, "That's a cow. A cow is a domestic animal. Cows eat grass. We get milk from cows." Another day the teacher puts on the board a list of wild animals, and the students volunteer statements. When, for example, the teacher points to a bear, the student responds, "That's a bear. A bear is a wild animal. Bears live in the forest. A bear is a very strong animal."

e. Similarly, on another day the teacher may put on the blackboard a wall chart or list of common flowers. She proceeds to ask questions about these flowers in the same way that she asked questions about domestic and wild animals. Later the students volunteer sentences about each of the flowers in the same way that they volunteered information about the animals.

f. In subsequent classes, the teacher can put on the blackboard lists or wall charts of (1) common vegetables, (2) common fruits, (3) articles of clothing, (4) dinnerware and silverware, (5) common foods, and (6) articles of furniture. Any common, everyday objects, grouped by categories, will provide the stimulus for simple classroom conversation. In each case, the teacher asks questions about the objects and engages in simple conversation with the students, based on the questions. Later, after the students have become familiar with the material, they volunteer three or four sentences about each of the objects indicated.

g. The teacher can use the classroom wall map to ask the students simple geographical questions about the various foreign countries appearing on the map. Some suggestions were made on page 70 about this technique of teaching classroom conversation.

h. The teacher can also stimulate classroom conversation through the use of a cardboard clock with movable hands. If a cardboard clock is not available, the teacher can draw a picture of a clock on the blackboard. She "sets" the clock and asks questions about telling time. She can later include related matters such as setting a clock, winding a clock, regulating a clock which runs fast or slow, etc. She can teach a great deal of useful vocabulary in this manner at the same time the students are getting necessary practice in conversation.

10. Other teachers prefer to set aside an even longer period for classroom conversation. Instead of a short ten or fifteen minute period each day, these teachers set aside a half-hour or even a full class hour, one day each week, for conversational purposes. This arrangement has some advantages over the shorter class sessions since it permits the teacher to introduce many new and different classroom activities, some of which may be interesting to the students. The system, however, will not work well with beginning students or even low intermediates. Students must have a fairly good knowledge of English to engage in conversational work for so long a time.

During this extended conversation period, students give oral reports. These reports may cover books which they have read, trips they have taken, or movies they have seen. Or the students may engage in simple debates which the teacher assigns beforehand. The class can orally read short one-act plays, with the students assuming the roles of the various characters. The teacher can also conduct various kinds of simple games. During a half-hour period, the girls can line up on one side of the room and the boys on the other side, and the teacher can conduct an old-fashioned spelling match. She can plan any number of interesting activities of this kind and present them during this extended, weekly conversational session.

The following simple procedure can be used effectively with an advanced class, especially where students are of mixed nationalities or come from different geographical regions. The teacher calls one student to the front of the class. This student sits in a chair, preferably close to the teacher's desk. Thus, the teacher is able to guide the discussion more easily and give the student some moral support. Each student in the class then asks *one* question to the student sitting in front. The questions can be on any subject. The only requirement is that the students make no grammatical errors in forming the questions. The student sitting in front answers each question. Frequently, the class encourages him to talk about his native country, his hometown, or his village. He tells about some of the unusual customs or traditions which prevail there. This procedure to stimulate conversation results in worthwhile classroom discussions.

CHAPTER V
THE TEACHING OF READING

In any modern language course where the chief emphasis is placed upon teaching the students to speak and understand English, reading assumes a somewhat secondary position. This does not mean that reading by itself is not important to the foreign student. In other circumstances the roles might well be reversed, with the teaching of reading becoming the chief aim of the course. Despite the present world-wide importance of English, there are still places where students have no actual contact with oral English. These students have no occasion to speak English at any time or even to hear English spoken. In classes for such students, it is almost foolish to spend time teaching the more difficult skills of understanding and speaking. It is simpler and more practical just to teach these students how to read.

The average student who is learning to speak English acquires an active or speaking vocabulary of some five or six hundred words after long months of continuous practice and drill. Within the same period, a student who is concentrating only on reading can acquire a passive or reading vocabulary of over a thousand words. A student who studies English in an oral language course must practice grammar forms over and over in drills and conversation before he can use these forms correctly. The student who studies English in a language course that has reading as its basis has only a passive knowledge of these grammar forms and probably cannot use them in oral conversation.

However, in an English course such as we have outlined

in this book, we must by necessity take the more difficult path of teaching oral English. As we explained earlier, the vast majority of students today wish to learn how to speak and understand English. Hence reading, like everything else in a language course, is subordinated to this purpose. Reading no longer becomes an end in itself. It serves simply as a means of providing students with additional oral practice. Students must naturally learn how to read English, but the value of reading is limited. We refer here, of course, to reading done in class, not to outside or collateral reading. As soon as they are ready for it, all students should be assigned as much outside reading as possible. In an oral system, however, reading in the classroom is confined to whatever material appears in the textbook. It is taught by oral means only. If, in the upper levels of study, a classroom reader is introduced, it is used in the same way, with strictly oral ends in view.

In using reading material as a means of providing students with additional practice in speaking and understanding English, the teacher asks various questions based on the reading material. From these questions, she leads the students into different avenues of simple conversation. Let us suppose that an intermediate class is reading a simple anecdote or fable from Aesop concerning a group of animals talking together among themselves in the forest about the popularity of the elephant. The teacher first introduces the reading material in any manner she prefers. Some teachers feel that it is more interesting to the class if the students themselves first read the material aloud. Other teachers feel that this is a poor technique and insist that all reading material be presented orally by the teacher first, in one form or another.

In any case, after the new material has been introduced, the teacher begins at once to question the students on this material and to encourage whatever classroom conversation may grow out of her questions. She may first direct one of the students to again read aloud the opening two or three lines of the anecdote. She herself then reads the same material aloud.

However, coming to the word *elephant,* she pauses and asks, "Is the elephant a large or a small animal?" After the first student has answered this question, she asks a second student, "Is the elephant larger or smaller than a horse?" She may ask a third student, "Have you ever seen an elephant?" Or she may ask, "Have you ever seen an elephant in the circus?" The circus generally interests most young people. Additional questions may therefore come from the word *circus.* Some simple classroom discussion may also result. If it does, the teacher encourages the discussion. If it does not, she simply returns to the text.

Returning to the text, the teacher directs another student to read the next two or three lines of the anecdote. The teacher repeats the reading of this same material. But, coming now to the word *popularity,* she proceeds to ask questions branching out from this word in the same way that she asked questions branching out from the word *elephant.* She asks questions such as, "Who is the most popular movie actor today?"; "Who is the most popular movie actress?"; and "What is the most popular sport in your country?"

Again, if this general subject matter proves interesting, the teacher pursues it, asking additional questions. If it does not prove interesting, she returns to the text. The class continues with the reading of the anecdote. The teacher at the same time continues to ask various questions based on the reading material. She also encourages whatever classroom discussion may develop as a result of her questions. When such discussion lags or fails to develop, she returns to the reading material.

This teaching technique is easy to use and requires simply a little practice on the part of the teacher. It often leads to fairly lively classroom discussion. In any event, it serves to provide students with considerable oral practice in answering the teacher's questions. Teachers who speak English natively can generally think up enough questions on the spot to utilize this technique effectively.

When teachers are unable to do this, they simply prepare the lesson beforehand. They pick out the words in the reading material on which they can base interesting questions. They then make up these questions and keep them in a notebook. Teachers who do not speak English fluently should naturally prepare all questions carefully beforehand. This technique can be used with any kind of reading material, providing the material is not difficult and falls within the vocabulary range of the students. All questions, of course, should be carefully graded so that the students can readily understand them.

CHAPTER VI
THE TEACHING OF VOCABULARY

It is not necessary to discuss the general subject of vocabulary in depth. First, we have no interest here in discussing the various theoretical aspects of English vocabulary. Some authorities give these matters considerable attention. They break down all words into various categories and then apply high-sounding, technical terminology to these categories. They also discuss at length the subject of vocabulary range, recommend the exact number of words to be taught at each level of English study, and so forth.

All of this is somewhat naive. English vocabulary is not so easily compartmentalized. It does not make much difference if we teach a few more words on one level and a few less on the next level. Other considerations, particularly practice and drill, are of far greater importance. Moreover, theoretical or philosophical discussions of vocabulary and related matters, though sometimes interesting, rarely help a teacher to teach any better.

Writers who indulge in such discussions often know little about the actual teaching of a foreign language. These experts, in too many cases, are grammarians, phoneticians, semanticists, specialists in English literature, all presuming today to be "linguistic scientists." Rarely have any of these experts taught English as a foreign language for any extended period of time. Moreover, many of them do not speak any foreign language fluently or know any foreign language well. Consequently, they understand few of the practical problems confronting the teacher who is teaching a foreign language or the student who is learning it.

As we explained at the beginning of this book, we are interested here mainly in talking about classroom procedures, in suggesting to teachers simple, everyday techniques which may serve to make their work more interesting and at the same time more effective. In the matter of vocabulary range, it is merely assumed that the teacher will follow the classroom textbook in deciding what vocabulary to teach. Most textbook writers today give considerable attention to this problem. They present all new vocabulary, as well as all new grammar and conversational patterns, in careful progression. Their judgment in these matters is to be trusted. When they diverge slightly on occasion from established frequency lists, they usually have good reasons for doing so.

Second, anyone who has read the three previous chapters covering the teaching of grammar, conversation, and reading will already have a good idea as to how vocabulary is taught in the type of modern language course which we recommend in this book. Words rarely exist by themselves. They are seldom used independently. They form part of a grammatical phrase or an idiomatic or conversational phrase. Thus, when we teach the oral use of grammar, we teach vocabulary at the same time. When we teach conversation and put stress on pattern practice, we are simultaneously teaching vocabulary since conversational patterns extend in many directions and involve a continuous use of new vocabulary. When we study reading, using it as the basis for oral drill and conversation, we are practicing new vocabulary. In brief, the same techniques which we use to teach grammar, conversation, and reading are used to teach new vocabulary. The method may almost be described as an inductive one. Emphasis is not placed directly upon the new vocabulary itself, but rather upon the grammatical or conversational phrase. Vocabulary is learned in the context of the entire phrase.

This does not exclude from consideration other techniques which individual teachers may also wish to employ. Some teachers use dictation regularly to implement the teaching of all new words. They may also use conventional methods, such as putting new words on the blackboard at the end of each lesson and then drilling the students on these words in various forms. The teacher may ask questions using the new words, or she may require that students make up original sentences with the new words. She may also assign the new words for study at home as part of the written assignment. The teacher may use any such technique which seems to give good results. She should abandon any technique which does not prove practical, regardless of any professional recommendations it may carry.

Here again we must keep in mind that the teaching of new vocabulary, like the teaching of any other phase of language, is a difficult and complicated task. There are no sure and easy ways of teaching new words. Nor are there any shortcuts to be taken. The teacher proceeds pragmatically, making use of whatever teaching technique seems most logical at the moment. Moreover, students vary greatly in their response to stimuli which will help them to remember vocabulary items. Consequently, in teaching any new vocabulary, the teacher should appeal to all the physical senses. The students should both hear and see all new words. They should have the opportunity to repeat aloud and write new words as many times as possible.

CHAPTER VII
THE TEACHING OF PRONUNCIATION

The teaching of English pronunciation is both a simple and a complicated procedure. It is simple in that such teaching involves merely the drilling of students on the various sounds of English. Any conscientious teacher who has good pronunciation can do this. She offers herself as a model of good pronunciation. She corrects as best she can any errors which the students make. For teachers who are not native speakers of English, the language laboratory is an almost essential aid. Such teachers should schedule regular laboratory periods so that their students will have the opportunity to hear native speakers and to use them as their models. Many of the tapes that accompany the standard texts include pronunciation exercises. In addition, there are supplementary tapes for drill on pronunciation.

The teacher should keep in mind at all times, of course, that ear training is extremely important in the teaching of any foreign language. Drill on the proper articulation of sounds is necessary, but ear training is even more fundamental. A student must first hear a sound clearly before he can reproduce it. Concepts of quality, pitch, and volume originate in the hearing area of the brain. The tonal image is heard mentally before it is actually produced by the voice. If this image is not exact, the production of the sound will not be accurate. Consequently, all pronunciation drills should be continued over as long a period of time as possible. The teacher should never jump from one exercise to another but should continue working on each individual sound until the sound is heard clearly by the students and the proper ear and hearing habits have been established.

It takes a much longer time than most teachers realize for a student to distinguish clearly the various sounds in a foreign language, particularly if such sounds do not exist in his own native language or are produced in a different way from comparable sounds in his own language. For example, a beginning student of English, whose native language is Spanish, is completely "deaf" to the difference between the English vowel sounds [ɪ] and [i] in such words as *bit* and *beat*. The difference is so clear to the English ear that it is hard to realize that anyone, regardless of language background, should have difficulty in hearing it. Yet to the Spanish-speaking student, *bit* and *beat* sound exactly alike. Moreover, it will take this student several months to hear any difference between the two words. After this, it will take him another six months before he can approximate the difference in his own speech. Finally, unless he is checked continually, he will regress later and just not bother to differentiate between the two sounds. This applies not only to [ɪ] and [i] but also to the difference between various other combinations of English sounds which frequently confuse foreign students. The teacher, consequently, must be untiring in her efforts to correct her students. She must also be ready to wait a long time to see any real improvement.

Still, as we have said, there is nothing particularly difficult about such teaching. It is sometimes hard work. But the teacher proceeds in a straightforward manner through the various English sounds. She simply encourages her students to imitate her own pronunciation.

On the other hand, as we have already mentioned, the teaching of pronunciation can also be a much more specialized task. If a teacher is to do more than simply guide her students through the various sounds, she should first understand some of the basic principles of English speech production. She should also be able to make use of these principles in her teaching. In this case, the effectiveness of her teaching does not depend so much upon the teaching methods or techniques which she employs but rather upon her knowledge and understanding of the general subject matter.

In this section on *Pronunciation,* we should like to discuss briefly some of the aspects of English speech which relate directly to the correction of errors in pronunciation.

Phonetics—The International Phonetic Alphabet.

Phonetics has been defined as the study of speech sounds and the art of pronunciation. Any teacher who attempts to teach pronunciation automatically makes some use of phonetics. The teacher's knowledge of theoretical phonetics may be very limited, but in correcting the accent of her foreign students, she unconsciously makes use of whatever she knows. She guides her students toward correct pronunciation through frequent drill. She makes a careful distinction between one sound and another. All of this is phonetics.

Naturally, the more a teacher knows about phonetics, the better. A well-trained teacher of any foreign language generally has taken one or more courses in speech training. Such a teacher knows something about the speech apparatus and something about speech production in general. She also has a general knowledge of the phonetic structure of English. A distinction should be made here, of course, between *phonetics* and *phonetic symbols.* These terms are not identical, although many people tend to use them indiscriminately. While phonetics is concerned with the study of speech sounds and proper pronunciation, phonetic symbols remain simply one of the tools which the phoneticist uses in analyzing language. It is quite possible to teach pronunciation without making use of phonetic symbols. It is also possible to make extensive use of such symbols without succeeding in teaching pronunciation.

The most common set of phonetic symbols now in use

are those which make up the alphabet of the International Phonetic Association. Most teachers of English as a foreign language are already familiar with this International Phonetic Alphabet (IPA). Phonetic symbols of this alphabet now appear, to a greater or lesser degree, in most modern textbooks. The alphabet was devised many years ago by a group of European phoneticists, the majority of whom were French. Generally, the language teacher's problem is to determine the extent to which she should make use of these IPA symbols in her own teaching.

There are certain groups who strongly advocate the extensive use of phonetic transcription in all foreign language teaching. These groups make great claims about the results to be achieved. In general, their arguments are sound. The theory underlying the use of phonetic symbols is simple and logical. The International Phonetic Alphabet provides a single symbol for each sound in the language. In English, for example, where the pronunciation of a word so often fails to accord with the spelling, we thus have a method of making the pronunciation clear. Particularly in cases where a student cannot pronounce a word or is confused by the obscuring of certain syllables, it is helpful to be able to transcribe the word into phonetic script. Also, in teaching certain of the vowel sounds, particularly those which are peculiar to English, it is useful to have at hand a symbol to represent these sounds. By means of phonetic symbols one can also indicate the voicing or unvoicing of terminal consonants, the existence of strong and weak forms, etc. These are all definite advantages.

Yet, despite these advantages, as one goes down through the ranks of practicing teachers, one finds considerable disenchantment with the entire phonetic system of transcription now in use. Many teachers have conscientiously tried to use the IPA system in their work, only to find that the results did not justify the time spent, first, in teaching the various symbols themselves and, second, in adapting these symbols to the many subtleties of everyday English speech. Moreover, attempts to simplify the IPA system have not been particularly successful. One group of authorities has sponsored one set of changes; another group has recommended something quite different. While the general tendency toward simplification is to be commended, such unrelated changes only add to the confusion already felt by many teachers regarding the use of phonetic symbols in general.

In many cases the problem is simply one of the classroom situation. It is easy to understand how the use of phonetic symbols may prove very effective in a well-organized school system where students begin to study English in the lower elementary grades and continue studying right through high school. In such classes there is both time and opportunity to make phonetics an integral part of the program. But in shorter, more intensive classes there is often little place for phonetic transcription. Many individual teachers are not sufficiently trained to use the IPA system effectively. Students in such classes often react unfavorably to learning and using phonetic symbols of any kind.

Specific complaints about the International Phonetic System of markings are many and varied. Native English-speaking teachers often wonder why they must use the rather strange symbol [ʃ] to indicate a sound which is adequately represented in English by the letters *sh* (as in *she*, *ship*, *push* etc.). Similarly, *ch* in English clearly represents the initial sound in *church* and *child*. It is a sound not easily confused with any other. Yet it must be rendered in phonetic transcription by the combination [tʃ]. The letter *y* stands in English for the initial sound in *yes* and *year*. In the IPA system, the sound is represented by [j] since in Teutonic languages this is the letter used to represent this sound. To the English eye, however [j] immediately suggests a quite different sound.

Finally, the phonetic symbols in current school use, without special qualifying markings, fail to indicate in any way important differences between the production of many English sounds and the production of the corresponding sounds in other languages. English *t*, for example, is not pronounced like Spanish *t*. English *p* is not pronounced

89

like Spanish *p*. The sounds *t, d, p, b, k, g* are all aspirated in English and produced with a slightly different tongue position from that used in Spanish. English *l* and English *r* have little similarity to Spanish *l* and Spanish *r*. Yet the phonetic symbols for *t, d, p, b, k, g, r, l* indicate no differences between the two corresponding sets of sounds. Consequently, the English-speaking person will give to these symbols his own English pronunciation, the Spanish-speaking person will give them a Spanish pronunciation, and each one will assume that he is pronouncing the sounds correctly in the foreign language. In this case, phonetic symbols not only fail to help the student. They do positive harm in tending to confirm the student's bad habits and faulty pronunciation.

Classification of Speech Sounds

There are twenty-six letters in the English alphabet, but there are upwards of some fifty different and distinct sounds. It is not our purpose here to describe all of these sounds or even to attempt to classify each of them. What follows below is merely a very general outline of the most important classe   of English sounds. Some of the terms defined here appear frequently in later discussions. It seems only logical, therefore, to describe such terms briefly at this point in order that the reader may understand more easily the material which follows. Any teacher who is interested in learning more about this general subject matter may refer to the various standard textbooks dealing with English speech.

The sounds of any language are generally divided into two main groups, vowels and consonants. All vowels are produced with the voice, that is, with vibration of the vocal cords. They differ from consonants in that the outward flow of sound is largely unrestricted. In consonants, this flow is interrupted or diverted by one of the articulators—teeth, tongue, lips, soft palate.

There are anywhere from eleven to sixteen vowels in English, depending upon their classification. That is, the number depends not upon their possible production within the speech apparatus but upon their classification by different phoneticians. Some writers on phonetics recognize three vowels in the *a* group and four in the mid-vowel group. More recent writers tend toward some simplification of these and other groups. Phoneticians further classify vowels as *front, middle,* and *back* vowels, depending upon the position of the tongue in the mouth during production. Thus, [i], [ɪ], and [e] are front vowels, the tongue being in high front position when they are produced. [u], [ʊ], and [o] are back vowels. [ə] and [ɚ] are middle vowels.

Consonants are classified according to the manner of articulation as follows: (1) Stops or plosives. In the production of these sounds, the breath is checked in its outward movement, then suddenly released with a slight explosion. In this group fall the sounds *p, b, t, d, k, g.* (2) Continuants. A continuant is a sound which may be "continued" or prolonged as long as the speaker has breath to sustain it. Continuants are further divided into nasals [m, n, and ŋ], laterals [l], and fricatives [f, v, h, w, θ, ð, s, z, ʃ, ʒ]. The *nasals* are produced by stopping the air in the mouth and emitting it through the nose. The only *lateral,* [l], is made by pressing the tip of the tongue against the upper tongue ridge and emitting the air at the sides of the tongue. *Fricatives* are breathing or hissing sounds caused by the narrowing or constriction of the vocal apparatus at some particular point.

A further classification of consonants concerns their production with voiced or with voiceless breath. This is an important classification for our purposes since the voicing or unvoicing of consonants, under certain specified conditions, is important in correcting pronunciation errors. *Voiced consonants* are produced with vibration of the vocal chords. In this group we have *b, d, g, l, ð, v, z, ʒ. Unvoiced consonants* are produced with breath alone. These include *p, t, k,* θ, *f, s, ʃ.*

It should be further observed that most voiced and unvoiced consonants fall into pairs, one consonant of the pair being voiced and the other unvoiced. Thus *b* is voiced; *p* is unvoiced—although both sounds are otherwise produced

91

alike. Such pairs may be grouped as follows.

Voiced	b	d	g	v	z	ð	ʒ
Unvoiced	p	t	k	f	s	θ	ʃ

Stress and Rhythm—Strong and Weak Forms

Stress is the emphasis given to a particular syllable within a word or to a particular word within a group of words. In individual words, stress is often referred to as *accent.*

In English, words are very strongly accented. The accented syllable receives greater force than in most languages. The unaccented syllables, in turn, receive correspondingly less force. This tendency in English results in various phonetic changes. In emphasizing the accented syllable so strongly, we automatically sacrifice the vowel values in the remaining unstressed syllables. *It may be stated as a principle in English that all vowels, when occurring in unstressed syllables, are reduced from their normal values to the level of the neutral vowel* [ə]. For example, in the words *attempt* [ətémpt], *contain* [kəntén], *recent* [rísənt], we can see clearly how this principle operates. The vowel of the unaccented syllable in each case is reduced from its normal value to the neutral [ə]. The only vowels which seem to resist this leveling tendency on occasion are the high front vowel [i] and the low back vowel [u]. Both these vowels are also reduced in unstressed syllables, but [i] is sometimes weakened only to [ɪ], as in *become* [bɪkə́m]; [u] is weakened to [ʊ], as in *July* [dʒʊláɪ].

This important principle of English speech is often difficult for the foreign student to understand. In his native language, the student is often taught to respect the quality of all vowels. So, in speaking English, he naturally assumes that if he pronounces each syllable clearly and exactly he will be better understood. Actually, the reverse is true.

92

Words in English are distinguishable by rhythm as well as by sound. Consequently, the student will be much better understood if he stresses the accented syllable strongly and totally obscures all the remaining vowels.

Although consonants do not have strong and weak forms, they also undergo changes in value, just as vowels do. They are subject to the influence of stress. They are also influenced particularly by neighboring sounds, undergoing a process known as *assimilation*. Thus one sound may be altered by the sound which follows it (progressive assimilation). Another sound may be altered by the sound which precedes it (regressive assimilation). In the word *looked*, for example, the final voiced d follows a breathed k. After pronouncing k, it is so much easier for us to leave the vocal cords in relaxed position rather than to draw them together sharply for the normal voicing of the d that we end up by unvoicing the d. The word, though still retaining its old spelling, is thus pronounced [lʊkt]. We shall come back to this particular type of assimilation when we consider in detail the voicing and unvoicing of final consonants.

Examples of assimilation may be seen in many common words. In the word *action*, originally pronounced [ǽktyən], the [t] has been drawn toward the back of the mouth by [y]. The [y], in turn, has become unvoiced because of the influence of the [t]. The result is that both consonants combine to produce the unvoiced sibilant [ʃ]. Thus the word is now pronounced [ǽkʃən]. This same assimilation occurs today in most words ending in *tion*. Similarly, *soldier* has been changed from [sóldyɚ] to [sóldʒɚ]. In words like *deserve* [dɪzɚ́v] and *observe* [ɑbzɚ́v] the [s] has become voiced because the vocal cords, in making the previous voiced sound, remain tense for the [s], thus changing it to its voiced form [z].

Assimilation is a very common process which occurs in all languages. It results from a simple *law of economy*, whereby the organs of speech, instead of taking a new position for each sound, tend to draw sounds together with the purpose of saving time and energy. Assimilation becomes important in teaching English to foreign students only when the teacher fails to understand its operation and importance. Many teachers tend to follow the spelling of words and to teach overly-precise forms rather than accepted assimilations. Thus, some teachers will teach *picture* as [pɪ́ktyʊr] rather than [pɪ́ktʃɚ]. By analogy they then teach *nature* as [nétyʊr] instead of [nétʃɚ], *literature* as [lɪ́tɚətyʊr] instead of as [lɪ́tɚətʃɚ]. They teach *educate* as [ɛ́dyʊket] rather than [ɛ́dʒəket]. These same teachers are likely to claim that *did you*, pronounced [dɪ́dʒʊ], or *don't you*, pronounced [dóntʃʊ] are vulgarisms to be avoided in careful speech. Yet these forms occur in their own speech and in the speech of everyone who speaks everyday, standard English. Students, therefore, should be acquainted with these and comparable assimilations. Even if they can't use them in their own speech, they should at least be able to recognize and understand them in the speech of others.

We read above that all words of more than one syllable are strongly accented in English. That is, one syllable receives considerable stress while the remaining syllables are weakened accordingly. *This same principle of accent holds true in phrases as well as in individual words.* In all phrases in English, one word or syllable is strongly accented. The remaining words or syllables receive correspondingly less stress. The vowels in all unstressed syllables are reduced from their original values to the neutral vowel [ə]. One-syllable words such as articles, conjunctions, and pronouns are reduced to their corresponding *weak forms*. The article *an* [æn], for example, is weakened to [ən]. The conjunction *and* [ænd] becomes [ənd]. *Can* [kæn] becomes [kən] or even [kn].

It is easy for students (and teachers) to understand the accenting of individual words, but rarely do they understand the comparable accenting of phrases or thought groups. Yet when we speak, we always speak in phrases or thought groups. It is quite natural that we should accent the main or content words in a sentence and subordinate the less important elements.

The following examples should help to show how this

principle applies in everyday speech. When in speaking we use any simple prepositional phrase such as *in the morning*, we do not pronounce each word or syllable separately. Nor do we give each syllable equal stress. Instead, we run all the words together to form a single element. We also subordinate all syllables to the one important and stressed syllable—[ɪnðəmɔ́rnɪŋ]. Similarly, in the verb phrase *they are leaving* we do not pronounce any of the words separately. We run them together. At the same time we accent the first syllable of *leaving* and subordinate all of the remaining syllables—thus [ðeɚlívɪŋ] or, more common still, [ðɛrlívɪŋ].

It so happens that almost any phrase in English can be compared in its accent to some individual word. Thus, the phrase *in the morning* is accented exactly like the word *economic* [ɪkənɑ́mɪk]. The phrase *he's leaving* [hizlívɪŋ] carries the same accent as the word *appearing* [əpírɪŋ]. *"I'll be there"* [aɪlbiðɛ́r] compares exactly in accent to *disappear* [dɪsəpír]. *"He's been working"* [hizbɪnwɚ́kɪŋ] is accented in the same way as the word *introduction* [ɪntrədʌ́kʃən]. A long list of such equally accented phrases and individual words can be drawn up by the teacher and used by the students for practice purposes.

Obviously, in special circumstances, one can alter the pattern of any phrase and emphasize a different word or syllable from the one normally stressed. If someone asks us, "Is the book *on* the table or *under* the table?" we might well reply, "ON the table," stressing *on* rather than the first syllable of *table*, which is usually stressed. But this is a special situation which does not concern us here. In normal, everyday colloquial speech all phrases carry a definite accent. Moreover, this accent, which grows out of the grammar of the language, is recurrent and stable. To the English ear, it is as clear and recognizable as the accent of any individual word. Finally—and this is a very important point—if any phrase is accented incorrectly, the error is just as great and just as obvious as when a word is accented on the wrong syllable.

Many times a foreign student, trying to be precise, will

say, for example, "I *am* busy," putting stress on *am* instead of on the first syllable of *busy*, where it normally goes. The resulting distortion is just as clear to the English ear (and just as confusing) as if the student, in pronouncing the word *Indiana* [ɪndiǽnə] mistakenly shifts the accent to the second syllable and says instead *InDIana* [ɪndíənə].

What we are discussing here is really rhythm. The succession of properly accented phrases in a sentence establishes what is known as the rhythm of a language. Rhythm is a definite and tangible aspect of language. Rhythm provides a kind of musical framework for language. More important still, it also helps to convey meaning. In many cases rhythm is as important in this respect as individual words or grammar.

The teacher may well ask how she should go about teaching stress and rhythm if they are so important. Clearly, she should not neglect more fundamental things to concentrate on stress and rhytym. Rhythm is a rather subtle matter. It is not easily grasped or appreciated by students, particularly on the elementary or lower intermediate levels. Yet there are a few obvious things which the teacher can do.

1. She can show the relationship between the accenting of many common phrases and individual words, as explained above. In this connection she should be sure to emphasize the fact that we speak in phrases, not words, and that all phrases carry a definite accent, just as words do.

2. She can also teach phrasing as part of the teaching of pronunciation. In reading practice sentences to the class, she can emphasize the stressing of accented syllables and the obscuring of vowels in unaccented syllables. The students, in repeating the sentences after her, should follow the same rhythm patterns which she has emphasized. In this way, the students come in time to "feel" certain of the patterns into which English rhythm naturally falls.

3. The teacher can make use of the device of rhyming, particularly in teaching contracted verb forms such as *I'm, you're, he's, we're, they're, I'll, she'll, we've,* etc. Students fail to contract many of these forms sufficiently. They pro-

nounce them as though they were composed of two syllables rather than a single syllable. The teacher can coun-
teract this tendency by showing that *I'll* rhymes with *pile*;
he's rhymes with *sneeze*; *I'm* rhymes with *time*; *we've*
rhymes with *leave*; and so on.

4. The teacher can show students how English rhythm
falls into certain definite patterns. These patterns grow out
of the grammar in such a way that in speaking, we naturally stress the so-called content words. These are usually
nouns, main verbs, and descriptive adjectives. In most sentences such words carry the burden of meaning. In turn,
we subordinate all function words, words which serve simply to define or show mood, direction, etc. The use of content words may be seen clearly in the speech of very young
children when they are just learning to talk. A child will
say, for example, "Man hit dog stick." An adult expresses
the idea more precisely by the use of additional function
words. Thus, in the same circumstances, the adult might
say, "That man across the street is hitting his dog with a
stick."

The following are generally considered functional words
in English and accordingly are unstressed:

1. *Definite and Indefinite Articles.* The indefinite article
a, sometimes pronounced artifically as [e], is reduced in
normal speech to [ə]. *An* [æn] becomes [ən] or, more often,
simply [n]. The definite article *the,* pronounced artifically
by some teachers as [ði], becomes [ðə] in everyday speech.
Very often, in a rapid phrase such as *in the book* [ɪnðəbʊ́k],
the *th* [ð] sound loses all voice and becomes just a glide
position between the preceding sound and the following
[ə] sound.

2. *Personal Pronouns.* Foreign students of English generally tend to stress all of the personal pronouns, including
all nominative, possessive, and objective case forms. From
the point of view of rhythm, this often represents a rather
serious error. For example, in an ordinary sentence such as
"He threw away his cigarette," the foreign student inevitably tends to stress both *he* and *his*. He seems to think that
such pronouns are somewhat important for identification

purposes. The native speaker feels that the identity of *he* has already been established and therefore does not stress either of these pronoun forms. *He*, being a pronoun, must have an antecedent which has already been expressed or at least implied from earlier conversation. Thus, it needs no stress. The use of *his*, moreover, is almost redundant. The subject of the sentence, *he*, naturally threw away *his own* cigarette. If he had thrown away someone else's cigarette, this fact would have been clearly stated and the appropriate pronoun introduced and stressed. The foreign student naturally cannot stop and analyze the stress value of every personal pronoun which he uses, but at least he can learn to curb his tendency to stress these pronouns on each and every occasion.

3. *Auxilary Verbs*. Auxiliary verbs form a very essential part of English verb structure and are used widely to establish both tense and mood. Consequently, the foreign student thinks that they should always be expressed clearly. The native speaker, however, glides over most auxiliary verbs quickly, subordinating them to what he considers more important elements in the sentence. Too, he relies on the rhythm of the resulting verb phrases to convey his meaning. In the case of the auxiliary verbs *have, has, will, would, am, is, are,* the lack of stress is carried to the extreme where recognized contracted forms result—so-called *contractions*. Thus, *I am* becomes *I'm. I have* becomes *I've. She will* becomes *she'll. He would* becomes *he'd*—and so on.

4. *Miscellaneous*. In this category fall the various connecting words *and, but, or*—also the subordinate conjunctions *where, when, while, if, although* etc. All of these are unstressed. All prepositions are normally unstressed. The relative pronouns *who, which*, and *that*, since they are used simply to show relationships, are also considered functional words and are unstressed. These relative pronouns, when used as direct objects of the verb, are not only unstressed but frequently dropped altogether from the sentence in colloquial speech. Thus, "The mán *whŏm* Ĭ sáw" becomes "The mán Ĭ sáw." "The boók *which* Ĭ neéd" becomes "The

book Ĭ neéd." The rhythm patterns here remain substantially the same even after *whom* and *which* have been dropped from the sentences. This rhythm serves to sustain the meaning even though the relative pronouns have been eliminated.

Intonation

Intonation is the term used to describe the pitch or melody pattern of any group of words. The group of words involved is sometimes known as the "intonation group." Pitch, in case the term is not familiar to the reader, is the position of a note on the musical scale. Pitch is determined by the frequency of vibration at which air waves strike the ear drum.

Very often, when there is an increase of stress on any one syllable, there is an accompanying rise in pitch on the same syllable. However, one should be careful to distinguish clearly between stress and pitch. Stress is associated with rhythm. Variations in stress give rise to rhythm in language. Stress patterns and the resultant rhythm, as we have seen, grow out of the grammar of a language. Thus rhythm is stable and fairly predictable.

Changes in pitch, on the other hand, result in varying intonation patterns. Pitch is often a personal or individual matter, especially on advanced levels. Pitch and the resultant intonation thus show great variation in form. In addition, they frequently carry various emotional overtones.

There has been, in recent years, a great deal of attention given to pitch and intonation in the teaching of English as a second language. Some modern texts are literally full of all kinds of strange up and down markings designed to plot the various intonation patterns of English speech. This attention to a subject which on the other hand is very simple and on the other is too subtle and complex for analysis—even by experts—seems quite illogical.

In its more elementary form, pitch is very easy to observe and understand. We can clearly see how it operates in a single word. For example, in answer to a question as to when we are leaving, we might answer in a matter-of-fact tone, "Now." In such a case the voice trails off at the end of the word. The intonation is said to fall. This gives to the listener the idea that the speaker has finished speaking. On the other hand, if someone asks us to do something which we are not disposed to do immediately, we might answer, "Now?" Here the pitch is heightened and the intonation is said to rise. The listener immediately knows that a question is being asked. Some emotion may also be involved. This rise and fall of intonation may apply to phrases as well as to individual words. It also occurs in whole sentences, the intonation rising and falling with the various phrases or "intonation groups" which make up the sentence.

Clearly, there is no particular problem of understanding here. Meaning is conveyed, but in a definite and assured way. Generally, the same principles of pitch apply in all languages. Any student learning English, therefore, will follow these same intonation patterns naturally. If he fails to do so, it does not mean that he does not understand them. Probably he is too engrossed with remembering the right words and the correct grammar forms to give much attention to intonation. Later, when he gains control over these other elements, his intonation will automatically take a more natural form.

The following two principles govern all basic intonation patterns in English. These two principles are really all any foreign student needs to know about intonation and all he needs to be taught:

1. The first principle requires that all completed statements, including commands, end with a downward glide of the voice on the last accented syllable. Questions beginning with interrogative words such as *When, Where, Why,* since these words in themselves indicate that the statement is a question, generally follow this principle:

Complete statement: <u>My father is a lawyer.</u>

Command: <u>Please close the window.</u>

Questions beginning with question words:

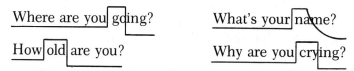

Where are you going?   What's your name?

How old are you?   Why are you crying?

2. The second principle is that all statements indicating incompleteness, doubt, or hesitation end with an upward glide of the voice on the last accented syllable. In this category are included all questions which may be answered by *yes* or *no*.

Are you going to school?

Does she speak Spanish?

To go beyond these two simple principles in teaching intonation to foreign students is simply to belabor the subject. Some diligent teachers, encouraged by certain professional groups, seem carried away by intonation. They plot out all kinds of intricate intonation patterns, assign numbers to each pattern, drill students up and down on various pitch levels. Frankly, much valuable class time, which can better be spent on more fundamental matters, is lost in this way.

In most cases intonation is entirely too personal, subtle, and complex a matter for classroom consideration. Different people speaking the same sentence will follow quite distinctive intonation patterns, depending upon their character, ulterior motives, state of health, or mood at the moment. A simple sentence such as "This is a book" may be expressed in a variety of ways just by raising or lowering the pitch on any one of the four words. One may say, "THIS is a book," raising the pitch on *this* and suggesting that *this*, finally, is a real book among books. Or one can turn the statement into an ironical question by raising the voice at the end of the sentence and asking, "This is a book?" Here the suggestion is that the book is so poor that it does not even deserve designation as a book.

However, these are considerations for the student of elocution or for someone entering upon a stage career, rather than for the foreign student studying English. It is no doubt true that the foreign student fails to show any great variety of intonation in speaking English, but this is no reason why he should be drilled on subject matter so remote from his immediate needs. There are hundreds of things which the beginning student does not do well in learning English. Teachers, therefore, should learn to teach each thing in its turn, first things first and last things last.

Intonation, if studied in detail, is subject matter for very advanced students only. The beginning or even intermediate student has all he can do to recognize the basic sounds of the foreign language, let alone pay attention to its various intonation patterns. A simple introduction to intonation can be presented on the lower levels, but it is senseless to treat intonation as extensively as some authorities now recommend. These authorities are inevitably teachers of speech or phonetics, theorizing about their own native language, *English*. They have no real experience teaching English as a foreign language.

Some teachers, to be sure, may argue that they have actually succeeded in teaching beginning students the proper intonation on simple phrases such as "Good Morning!", "How are you?", and "I am opening the book." But this means nothing at all. The students are totally unable to transfer this knowledge to other English phrases. Teaching complex intonation patterns to beginning and intermediate students may well be compared to teaching advanced mathematics to young children who have not yet learned to add or subtract.

Aspiration

Aspiration is the term given to the slight puff of air, like an [h], which follows the production of [p], [t], and [k] in English. This aspiration is strongest when [p], [t], and [k] are in initial position and followed by a vowel, as in the word *pen* [pɛn]. It is next strongest when the sounds are in final position, as in *map* [mæp]. It is weakest when the sounds occur in medial position; here the puff of air is so slight as to be hardly perceptible, as in *happy* [hæpi].

This aspiration is not a fundamental part of these sounds, which are all voiceless plosives. As may be seen from what has just been said, the aspiration varies in intensity with the position of the sound. When [p], [t], or [k] are followed by a consonant in the same breath group, the puff does not occur at all; for example, *pride* [praɪd]. Yet the aspiration remains a very important characteristic of each of these sounds, especially if the sound is in initial position. For one thing, the aspiration serves to distinguish the sounds from their voiced cognates [b], [d], and [g]. The sound [p], for example, is more than merely the unvoiced counterpart (cognate) of [b]. It is unvoiced [b], with a distinctive aspiration added, and this aspiration is clearly noticeable to the English ear and helps substantially in identifying the sound.

The same aspiration of these sounds does not occur in German, in the Slavic languages, or in any of the Romance languages. Consequently most foreign students studying English pay little attention to it. Generally, the student does not hear the aspiration clearly. Even in cases where he may hear it, he is unable to reproduce it. Yet no error is more noticeable in the speech of foreign students. It is an error which clings to the speech of even the most advanced students.

To the person not trained in speech, the difference between an aspirated [t] and an unaspirated [t] may not seem a very significant one. Yet the failure to aspirate comes through very clearly in English speech, causing a heavy, blunt effect which is definitely nonEnglish. Compare the pronunciation of *ten* (the numeral) in English and *ten* (the imperative form of *tener*) in Spanish. There sometimes resulting a definite confusion of words if the necessary aspiration is lacking. In rapid speech, unaspirated [p] sounds like voiced [b]; unaspirated [t] sounds like [d]; unaspirated [k] like [g]. The foreign student says *ten*, without aspirating the [t], and the native listener thinks he is saying *den*. The foreign student says *pie* and it sounds to his native listener like *by*.

This error, in general, is fairly easy to correct once the teacher understands the principle involved and the facts are made clear to the students. The teacher should first show the students how strong the aspiration of [p], [t], and [k] is in her own speech. She should pass among the students repeating such words as *pen, ten, come*. She can exaggerate slightly the aspiration of [p], [t], and [k], though this is not really necessary since the aspiration of these sounds, even in normal speech, is considerable. She can let students feel with the backs of their hands the strong puff of air which is emitted from her mouth each time she pronounces [p], [t], and [k]. Students are usually amazed at the really strong aspiration given to these sounds. Or the teacher can hold a small piece of paper lightly in front of her mouth as she speaks. The paper will flutter each time she says [p], [t], or [k]. A match flame, held before the mouth, shows the same effect.

After this, it is just a matter of practice on the students' part to learn this important principle of aspiration. Students should repeat aloud simple words beginning with [p]—*pen, pay, pour, put, pear*. Later they should practice with simple words beginning with [t] and [k]. At first, students can hold pieces of paper in front of their mouths to show the amount of aspiration taking place. However, this soon becomes unnecessary because the sharp difference between the aspirated and unaspirated forms of these sounds is presently clear to all. From this point on, it is just a matter of correction each time a student fails to aspirate [p], [t], or [k] sufficiently. There is, incidentally, little danger of over-aspirating these sounds. The effect of aspiration is very pleasant to the English ear. It is often thought that the stronger the aspiration, the more refined a person's speech is considered to be. Professional actors and actresses sometimes practice for hours to achieve a strong but precise aspiration on each [p], [t], and [k].

Voicing and Unvoicing of Final Consonants

Another serious error of the foreign student learning English is his failure, in required circumstances, to voice final consonants. We have already learned the difference between voiced and unvoiced consonants. The particular voiced consonants which concern us here are [b,d,g,v,z, ð,ʒ,dʒ]. Their unvoiced counterparts are [p,t,k,f,s,θ,ʃ,tʃ].

Sometimes in rapid speech it is difficult to tell whether a consonant is voiced or unvoiced. This simple test may be used. Stop the ears while sounding alternately any such pairs as *fife* and *five*, prolonging the final sounds of *f* and *v*. In holding the sound *f* by itself, one will hear only a fricative rustling of the breath as it passes the teeth and lips. In sounding *v*, this same friction is heard with the addition of voice, the vibration of the vocal cords.

In English, all voiced consonants occurring at the end of a word are generally held and voiced.* In German and the Slavic and Romance languages, the opposite situation prevails. All voiced consonants, when occurring in terminal position, are automatically unvoiced. For example, in Russian the name *Chekhov*, although terminating in *v*, a voiced consonant, is pronounced [tʃékɔf]. In accordance with the rules of Russian, the final *v* is automatically unvoiced and changed into its unvoiced counterpart *f*. In English this same word would normally be pronounced [tʃékɔv]. The final *v* would be held and voiced. Compare English pronunciation of *love* [ləv], *move* [muv], and *of* [əv].

The foreign student, in bringing to English the habits of speech acquired in his own native language, naturally tends to unvoice all final voiced consonants. The effect in English, however, is unfortunate. The student, instead of saying *his* [hɪz], says [hɪs]. Instead of saying *have* [hæv], he says [hæf]. For *bag* [bæg], he says [bæk], and so on. The list of such possible distortions, where the foreign student turns final *d* into *t*, final *g* into *k*, final *v* to *f*, and so

*Final voiced consonants are occasionally unvoiced in English through the process of assimilation. See page 93.

105

forth, is almost endless. In some cases, actual confusion of words results. If a student, in pronouncing *bad*, unvoices the final *d* and changes it to *t*, he comes out with *bat*. In such a case, he has changed not only the form of the word but also its meaning. There are many pairs of English words distinguishable only by the voicing or unvoicing of the final consonant. Consider, to name just a few: *bed, bet; need, neat; feed, feet; buzz, bus; grows, gross; rise, rice; raise, race; pays, pace; leave, leaf; bag, back.*

Evidently, it is very important to hold and voice all such final voiced consonants in English. This voicing sometimes varies in intensity, but this fact need not concern the foreign student. The principles involved should first be explained to the student so that he understands what he is doing. Then he should be drilled carefully on matching pairs of words such as those which appear above. He should also be given practice with phrases and short sentences containing final voiced consonants. It is sometimes helpful if it is explained to the student that all vowels preceding final voiced consonants are somewhat lengthened in duration. That is, all vowels are held slightly longer before final voiced consonants than before final unvoiced consonants. The [æ] in *bad*, for example, is of longer duration than the [æ] in *bat*. The [ɛ] in *bed* is held longer than the [ɛ] of *bet*, etc.

General Suggestions and Remarks

As mentioned earlier, we are not interested here in discussing individual sounds, such subject matter being the province of the conventional textbook on speech. In the limited space allowed us, we cannot consider in detail even those sounds which give foreign students particular difficulty. However, any teacher teaching English to foreign students for only a short time knows what sounds these are. She can give comparison drills to clarify the difference, for example, between [ɪ] and [i], [ɛ] and [æ], [o] and [ɔ], to name just a few of the combinations which foreign students often confuse. She can give additional exercises for

106

ear training, so that students are enabled to hear each of the sounds clearly.

In conclusion, however, we should like to speak briefly of a few sounds which sometimes prove troublesome even to the conscientious and experienced teacher. Again, these remarks are of a practical rather than a theoretical nature.

In English, the sound of [l] has two forms, generally designated as the clear [l] and the dark [l]. The clear [l] is used at the beginning of a word or after an initial consonant. Examples are *low, glow*. The dark [l] is used at the end of a word or before a final consonant. Examples are *fall, fold*. In both forms the tip of the tongue is pressed against the gum ridge. In the clear [l], however, the back of the tongue curves downward. In the dark [l] the back of the tongue is raised toward the soft palate. The difference in acoustical effect is quite pronounced.

The pronunciation problem here arises from the fact that most foreign students use the clear [l] in all positions. Their pronunciation of such common words as *all, fall, will, tell, fill, feel, bell, smell, call* is inevitably faulty. Consequently, the teacher must make clear the necessity of raising the back of the tongue on all final l's in English. By way of explanation she should prolong the sound of final [l] in all of the words above, making clear the difference in acoustical effect between this dark [l] and the clear [l] used in initial position. (If possible, she should compare Spanish pronunciation of *el*, the definite article, and English pronunciation of some comparable word such as *tell*, prolonging the final *l* in both cases.)

Some foreign students use what is known as an inverted or retroflex *l* in all positions. This *l* is formed with the tip of the tongue turned back toward the soft palate. The tendency toward using this *l* can generally be corrected by having students pronounce such words as *battle, shuttle, bottle*. As the *t* of these words is pronounced, the tongue should not be retracted but held in the same position. With the tip of the tongue, therefore, still against the gum ridge, the *l* should then be produced. Again, however, the back of the tongue must be raised.

[s] Terminal s, added to nouns to obtain the plural form and to verbs to form the third person singular of the present tense, often gives foreign students considerable difficulty. Es, rather than s, is added to all words ending in a sibilant sound (s, sh, ch, x, z) in order to make the pronunciation easier. The es is then pronounced as a separate syllable: churches [tʃə́tʃəz], teaches [títʃəz], wishes [wíʃəz]. If s is added to a word ending in a vowel sound or voiced consonant, the s becomes voiced by process of assimilation and is pronounced as z: finds [faɪndz], runs [rənz], trees [triz]. If, however, s is added to a word ending in an unvoiced consonant, the s remains unvoiced and is pronounced like s: hats [hæts], meets [mits].

It should be noted, in addition, that in many English words containing s in medial position, the s remains unvoiced and is pronounced as s. Examples are master [mǽstɚ], last [læst]. In others, it is voiced and pronounced like z. Examples are busy [bízi], reason [rízən]. Since English spelling gives no indication in any of these words as to how the s is to be pronounced, the foreign student is naturally confused. Generally, he uses unvoiced s in all positions. For busy [bízi], he says [bísi]. For reason [rízən], he says [rísən]. No error is more common in the speech of foreign students. None needs more vigorous attention on the part of the teacher. Most students need long and continuous drill, first in order to hear the voiced s [z] clearly and then to be able to produce it accurately in all positions, initial, medial, and terminal.

[θ] and [ð]   Both these sounds established themselves long ago as formidable enemies of the foreign student. The sounds exist in few foreign languages. They are also rather tricky to produce. However, this is not the problem we wish to point out here. Any conscientious teacher with sufficient time and application can teach these sounds adequately, showing the voiced quality of [ð] and the voiceless quality of [θ]. Many teachers, however, teach beginning student these sounds by having them put the tip of the tongue between the teeth, rather than behind the gum ridgewhere it properly belongs. These teachers apparently feel that it is easier for students to learn these new sounds in this way.

Unfortunately, many students continue indefinitely to form both *th* sounds with the tongue between the teeth. Esthetically, the picture of a student ejecting and withdrawing the tongue rapidly each time he makes a *th* sound is not a pretty one.

Moreover, the sounds [θ] and [ð] cannot be properly articulated with the tongue between the teeth. There is entirely too much tongue activity involved in placing the tongue in this position, with a consequent loss of time and effort. To form a good *th,* the tongue is held high in the mouth. Only the tip operates, rapidly and skillfully. The main body of the tongue does not move. Under no circumstances does the tongue ever emerge from the mouth.

A high tongue position, incidentally, seems to be an important factor in the production of many English sounds. This fact has not been generally emphasized by phoneticians. Yet [t, d, s, z, θ, ð, ʃ, ʒ, n, r, and l] are best produced in English with the tongue high in the mouth. The tip of the tongue and the blade provide the activity. The articulation of many foreign students shows a low tongue position. There is also considerable muscular weakness in the use of the tongue tip, which too often lies fixed in the bottom of the lower jaw and scarcely moves during speech production. In the native language of these students, a mid-tongue-teeth contact serves to form many of the important consonants.

[r] Another sound giving the foreign student considerable difficulty is *r.* We refer here to *r* used in initial position or following an initial consonant. Examples are *red, bread.* Final or post-vocalic *r* presents no particular problem. For initial *r,* however, the foreign student generally uses either a uvular *r,* made by vibration of the uvula, or the trilled *r* of Spanish and Italian. Neither of these sounds exists normally in English. They both sound excessively strong and vibrant to the English ear.

Phoneticians seem to disagree on the exact formation of *r* in English. It is really a glide sound, sometimes having a consonant quality and sometimes a vowel quality, depending upon accompanying sounds. It is produced with the tongue high in the mouth. The sides of the tongue are placed against the back teeth ridges. The middle of the tongue is slightly lowered or grooved, forming a narrow channel through which the breath stream passes. Some authorities claim that the tip of the tongue is slightly inverted. They also claim that the sound always originates with a motion toward the back of the mouth. Both these notions seem quite absurd. There is nothing retroflex about English *r*. Furthermore, it is precisely this backward motion that the foreign student must learn to avoid.

English *r* (or at least American *r*) is essentially a forward sound. It is best produced from the same elevated tongue position used for such sounds as [t, d, θ, ð, s, z, etc.], described above. There is also considerable lip activity involved. Acoustically, the sound is closely related to *w*. Proof of this is the fact that young children, when first learning to speak, often confuse the two sounds. They pronounce *rose* [roz] as [woz] and *rabbit* [rǽbət] as [wǽbət].

Students should be drilled on producing *r* in forward position. Pairs of words such as *weed-read, wed-red* should be practiced. The vibration of the lips on these pairs should be strongly emphasized so as to give students the "feel" of the lip activity involved. Other pairs of words such as *price-rice, bright-right* should also be practiced. With these pairs, students should be instructed to hold the same general position of tongue, teeth, and lips for the *r* as for the initial labials *p* and *b*. In other words, after the *p* and *b* are pronounced, there should be no motion backwards. Instead, the *r* should be produced in the same forward position used for *p* and *b*. Long practice and drill are often necessary to effect these changes in the production of *r*. Yet the transformation in the student's speech, once he is able to substitute this English *r* for the uvular, flapped, or trilled *r* of his native language, is often quite remarkable.

DIXSON'S BOOKS FOR TEACHING AND LEARNING ENGLISH

Alphabetical Arrangement of Titles

BEGINNING LESSONS IN ENGLISH (New Revised Edition) — An elementary text which directly and effectively will help beginners to speak English. Consists of pronunciation and conversation practice and grammar exercises.

COMPLETE COURSE IN ENGLISH (New Edition) — Books 1, 2, 3, and 4 — An ideal program for teaching English as a second language. Suitable for high school, college, and adult education classes. Contains dialogues, grammar explanations and exercises, and reading passages and conversation sections. Recordings are available on tapes or cassettes.

CURSO COMPLETO EN INGLES (New Edition) — Libros 1, 2, 3, & 4 — Identical to *Complete Course in English,* except grammar rules are stated in Spanish. For Spanish-speaking students who need to use some Spanish while learning English. Complete English-Spanish vocabulary lists. Recordings are available on tapes or cassettes.

CURSO PRACTICO DE PRONUNCIACION DEL INGLES (Clarey and Dixson, adapted by Julio Andújar) — Intended to help native Spanish speakers to develop good English pronunciation. Each lesson focuses on a single sound. Includes special exercises on intonation and phrase and sentence stress. Recordings are available on records or tapes.

EASY READING SELECTIONS IN ENGLISH (Revised Edition) — Absorbing short stories, simplified and adapted for intermediate and advanced students. Includes questions and exercises for conversation practice. Sequel to *Elementary Reader in English*. Recordings are available on tapes or cassettes.

ELEMENTARY READER IN ENGLISH (Revised Edition) — Articles, short stories, and anecdotes, simplified and adapted for beginning students. Vocabulary range — 1,000 words. Includes exercises in comprehension, conversation, and vocabulary. Recordings are available on tapes or cassettes.

EL INGLES EN ACCION — Elementary text stressing the oral aspect of learning. Instructions and grammar explanations in Spanish. Numerous exercises and review sections. Pocket-sized. Liberal use of pictures.

ENGLISH IN ACTION — Identical to *El Inglés en Acción* but with complete text in English.

ENGLISH STEP BY STEP WITH PICTURES (Revised Edition) — Beginner's text utilizing pictures as aids in learning. Vocabulary range approximately 800 words. Posters are now available.

ESSENTIAL IDIOMS IN ENGLISH (Revised and Explained) — Introduces basic idioms through extensive practice exercises. Contains approximately 600 high-frequency idioms. Divided into elementary, intermediate, and advanced levels. Appendix includes Spanish, French, and German equivalents for each idiom.

EVERYDAY DIALOGUES IN ENGLISH (Revised Edition) — Advanced conversation book with drills and exercises. Contains 41 dialogues on everyday situations and problems. Recordings are available on cassettes or tapes.

EXERCISES IN ENGLISH CONVERSATION (Revised Edition) — Books 1 and 2 — Complete course in conversational English. Graded lessons include dialogues or short readings, oral exercises, and review sections. Recordings are available on tapes or cassettes.

GRADED EXERCISES IN ENGLISH (New Revised Edition) — Numerous graded exercises arranged in topical form. Defines grammatical principles clearly. Presents each part of speech in its different forms. Answer Booklet available on request.

GRADED READERS (Revised Editions) — Ten American Classics simplified and adapted for greater reading pleasure. The vocabulary range of Book 1 is approximately 750 words. Each succeeding book adds about 200 new words. Book 10 includes approximately 2,600 words. Recordings are available on tapes or cassettes.

Book 1—*House of the Seven Gables*
Book 2—*Moby Dick*
Book 3—*Murders in the Rue Morgue and The Gold Bug*
Book 4—*The Pathfinder*
Book 5—*Outcasts of Poker Flat, Luck of Roaring Camp and Other Stories*
Book 6—*The Hoosier Schoolmaster*
Book 7—*The Portrait of a Lady*
Book 8—*The Rise of Silas Lapham*
Book 9—*Adventures of Huckleberry Finn*
Book 10—*The Red Badge of Courage*

HANDBOOK OF AMERICAN IDIOMS AND IDIOMATIC USAGE (Revised and Explained) — Lists and defines more than 5,000 of the most common words and phrases. Uses each idiom in an illustrative sentence.

INGLES PRACTICO SIN MAESTRO (Whitehouse and Dixson; New Edition) — Self-instructional program in English for native Spanish speakers. Includes twenty graded lessons. Instructions and explanations in Spanish. Recordings are available on records, tapes, or cassettes.

LAS 2,000 PALABRAS USADAS CON MAS FRECUENCIA EN INGLES — Handy pocket-sized booklet. Can be used for learning new vocabulary and reviewing or checking pronunciation and spelling. Includes Spanish equivalents of all English vocabulary words.

MI PRIMER DICCIONARIO ILUSTRADO DE INGLES (Dixson and Fox; New Edition) — Beginning word book for very young Spanish speakers learning English. Beautifully illustrated in full color. Includes Spanish equivalents of words and sentences in both Spanish and English. Total of 650 words.

MODERN AMERICAN ENGLISH (Revised Edition) — Books 1-6, Workbooks 1-6, Skillbooks 1-6, Teacher's Manuals (2) for Books 1-3 and 4-6 — Complete course for junior and senior high school students. Emphasizes verbal communication but also concentrates on reading and writing. Lessons graded according to difficulty. Recordings on tapes or cassettes and posters are available.

MODERN SHORT STORIES IN ENGLISH (Revised Edition) — Seventeen modern short stories by well-known American authors. For advanced students. Recordings are available on tapes or cassettes.

ORAL PATTERN DRILLS IN FUNDAMENTAL ENGLISH — Pattern drills on every major aspect of English grammar. Recordings are available on tapes.

PRACTICE EXERCISES IN EVERYDAY ENGLISH — A drill and exercise book for advanced students. Lessons are graded and extensive practice is given in grammar and idiomatic usage. Free answer booklet available with class orders.

PRONUNCIATION EXERCISES IN ENGLISH (Clarey and Dixson) — Variety of exercises treating every important English sound. Indispensable for improvement of pronunciation.

REGENTS ENGLISH WORKBOOKS 1-2-3 — Contain carefully planned exercises in grammatical structure, idiomatic usage, and vocabulary building. Also includes exercises in pronunciation, spelling, and punctuation.

RESUMEN PRACTICO DE LA GRAMATICA INGLESA (Dixson and Andújar) — A thorough guide to English grammar and syntax. Simple, straightforward Spanish explanations.

SECOND BOOK IN ENGLISH (Revised Edition) — Continuation of the materials presented in *Beginning Lessons in English.* Suitable for students on the intermediate level. Includes new vocabulary, extended reading and conversation exercises, and additional grammar practice.

SOUND TEACHING (Boggs and Dixson) — Audio-lingual course for conversation practice. Can be used as a complete course in itself or as a supplement to any English program. Recordings on tape are available.

TESTS AND DRILLS IN ENGLISH GRAMMAR (Revised Edition) — Books 1 and 2 — Practical drill books covering the entire field of English grammar. Emphasis on constant drill and repetition. Comprehensive review material with each lesson.

THE U.S.A.—THE LAND AND THE PEOPLE —
Elementary reader dealing with different regions of
the United States and describing the men and events
that helped to shape these regions.

THE U.S.A.—MEN AND HISTORY (Dixson and
Fox; Revised Edition) — Historical profiles of
twenty-five famous American men and women. An
intermediate reader.

DIXSON'S BOOKS FOR TEACHING AND LEARNING SPANISH

GRADED EXERCISES IN SPANISH (Andújar and Dixson) — Practice and drill material of all kinds. Structures and vocabulary introduced progressively. For use as a basic text, a practice book at first or second levels, or a review text at more advanced levels.

METODO DIRECTO DE CONVERSACION EN ESPAÑOL (Angel and Dixson; Revised and Updated) — Libros 1 & 2 — Teaching basic Spanish conversation in secondary schools, colleges, and adult classes. Graded dialogues and reading selections. Numerous exercises. Spanish-English vocabulary. Correlated with *Tests and Drills in Spanish Grammar*.

TESTS AND DRILLS IN SPANISH GRAMMAR (Angel and Dixson) — Books 1 & 2 — Contain all essentials of Spanish grammar. For use as basic texts, for review work, or as a supplement to a conversation course. Correlated with *Método Directo de Conversación en Español*.

WORKBOOK IN EVERYDAY SPANISH (Andújar and Dixson; Revised Edition) — Books 1 & 2 — Intended to supplement any standard classroom text in the teaching of Spanish as a foreign language. Includes comprehensive review of grammar, exercises and drills, and a Spanish-English glossary.

ARRANGEMENT BY LEVELS OF DIXSON'S ENGLISH TEACHING TEXTS

ELEMENTARY LEVEL
General Texts

Beginning Lessons in English
Complete Course in English — Book 1
Curso Completo en Inglés — Libro 1
English Step by Step with Pictures
English in Action
El Inglés en Acción
Inglés Práctico sin Maestro
Modern American English — Books 1 & 2

Grammar

Tests and Drills in English Grammar — Book 1

Workbooks

Regents English Workbook — Workbook 1
Modern American English — Workbooks 1 & 2

Conversation

Exercises in English Conversation — Book 1
Direct English Conversation — Book 1

Readers

American Classics
    Book 1—House of the Seven Gables
    Book 2—Moby Dick
Elementary Reader in English
Modern American English — Skillbooks 1 & 2
The U.S.A.—The Land and the People

INTERMEDIATE LEVEL
General Texts

Second Book in English
Complete Course in English — Books 2 & 3
Curso Completo en Inglés — Libros 2 & 3
Modern American English — Books 3 & 4

Grammar

Graded Exercises in English
Tests and Drills in English Grammar — Book 2

Workbooks

Regents English Workbook — Workbook 2
Modern American English — Workbooks 3 & 4

Conversation

Direct English Conversation — Book 2
Exercises in English Conversation — Book 2

Readers

American Classics
    Book 3—Murders in the Rue Morgue and the
        Gold Bug
    Book 4—The Pathfinder
    Book 5—Outcasts of Poker Flat, Luck of Roaring
        Camp, and Other Stories
    Book 6—The Hoosier Schoolmaster
Modern American English — Skillbooks 3 & 4
The U.S.A.—Men and History

ADVANCED LEVEL

General Texts

Complete Course in English — Book 4
Curso Completo en Inglés — Libro 4
Modern American English — Books 5 & 6

Grammar

Practice Exercises in Everyday English

Workbooks

Regents English Workbook — Book 3
Modern American English — Workbooks 5 & 6

Conversation

Everyday Dialogues in English

Readers

American Classics
    Book 7—The Portrait of a Lady
    Book 8—The Rise of Silas Lapham
    Book 9—Adventures of Huckleberry Finn
    Book 10—The Red Badge of Courage
Modern American English — Skillbooks 5 & 6
Modern Short Stories in English

BOOKS OF A SUPPLEMENTARY NATURE

Pronunciation Exercises in English
Essential Idioms in English
Handbook of American Idioms and Idiomatic Usage
Oral Pattern Drills in Fundamental English
Sound Teaching — A Laboratory Manual of American English
Teacher's Manuals for the Modern American English series

BOOKS OF A SUPPLEMENTARY NATURE

391